Unveiling the path to Happiness

A TRUE STORY OF A YOUNG WOMAN'S EXPERIENCES TO
SELF-DISCOVERY, SELF-MASTERY, INNER PEACE AND HAPPINESS

MAYA LINKINOSKA

First published by Ultimate World Publishing 2020
Copyright © 2020 Maya Linkinoska

ISBN

Paperback - 978-1-922372-74-1
Ebook - 978-1-922372-75-8

Maya Linkinoska, has asserted her right under the Copyright, Designs and Patents Act 1988 to be identified as the author of this work. The information in this book is based on the author's experiences and opinions. The publisher specifically disclaims responsibility for any adverse consequences, which may result from use of the information contained herein. Permission to use information has been sought by the author. Any breaches will be rectified in further editions of the book.

All rights reserved. No part of this publication may be reproduced, stored in or introduced into a retrieval system, or transmitted in any form, or by any means (electronic, mechanical, photocopying, recording or otherwise) without the prior written permission of the author. Any person who does any unauthorised act in relation to this publication may be liable to criminal prosecution and civil claims for damages. Enquiries should be made through the publisher.

Cover design: Ultimate World Publishing, Graphics Ergun Kamit
Layout and typesetting: Ultimate World Publishing
Editor: Emily Riches

Ultimate World Publishing
Diamond Creek,
Victoria Australia 3089
www.writeabook.com.au

DEDICATION

My purpose in writing this book is to leave a legacy.

I dedicate this book to my ancestors, my future children, and grandchildren.

CONTENTS

Introduction	vii
Chapter 1: My Family	1
Chapter 2: My Childhood	5
Chapter 3: My Sister and I	9
Chapter 4: New Zealand Adventure	15
Chapter 5: London Calling	19
Chapter 6: Monica	25
Chapter 7: My Spiritual Healing Journey	31
Chapter 8: Saturn Return and Liberation	41
Chapter 9: Reconnecting with My Inner Gypsy on The Gold Coast	47
Chapter 10: Lost Identity, New Identity	55
Chapter 11: Dark Night of the Soul	59
Chapter 12: My Psychosomatic Therapy Journey	63
Chapter 13: My Yoga Journey and the Path to Inner Peace and Happiness	67
Chapter 14: The Path to Silence and Inner Peace	81
Chapter 15: Past Lives and Ancestral Healing	91
Chapter 16: Animal Communication and Self-Mastery	97
Chapter 17: India	101
Chapter 18: Soul Purpose and Realignment	105
Dreams, Goals and Values: The Next Five to Ten Years	111
References	113
About Maya	115

INTRODUCTION

This book is about love and the courage it takes to follow the path less travelled towards self-discovery and happiness. It's about the kind of love you find in the flow of rivers and waterfalls that are able to break through rocks and mountains; the kind of moving energy you find in the perfect surfing wave. I am a love child and there is no limit or boundaries to the things I do out of love. When we are moved by love, we can achieve anything. When we are moved by fear, our life is limited and controlled by an illusion. Fear is the veil of illusion and love is the beauty behind the veil.

My name, Maya, is a versatile name with many meanings in different languages. It can mean love, water, black magic, or illusion. There is also the Mayan civilization and the ancient Maya people. My parents named me Maya (Maja in my native language, Macedonian) because "Maj" is the month of May and I was due to be born in May. However, I was born two weeks early, in April. Regardless of my early arrival, my parents still called me Maja.

I was born in Skopje, the capital of Macedonia, in Southeastern Europe. It is a landlocked country surrounded and protected by mountains, with many rivers and lakes. One famous person that was also born in my city is Mother Teresa. She stands for love and humanitarianism. My favourite quote of hers is:

> *"If you judge people, you have no time to love them."*[1]

My purpose here on Earth is to shine my light and share my love and wisdom: to help create heaven here on Earth. I am a spiritual life coach, healer, teacher, and artist. I live a dual life, like a medium, between worlds and different dimensions. My mission is to bridge the gap between heaven and earth, removing the veil which prevents many humans from experiencing life and love to the fullest.

I always knew I would be an author one day. Since my early childhood, I have had a passion for writing, reading, and books. I like to remain traditional: even though everything is available online these days, I still buy books and read the physical copy. The changing technology and evolution of ebooks will never change my passion for books. I love the smell and feel of books, the excitement of turning over the pages to see what's coming next. Writing makes me feel like I am right at home. I can lose myself in bookshops and libraries. I had a home library in my bedroom when I was a child.

I remember the first short story I wrote in primary school was published in the school newspaper. It was a descriptive story about spring. After that, I wrote many more short stories and poems. I love spring and the seasonal changes. As I said, I was born in April, which is spring in my place of birth. Spring is a season for change and rebirth: the time that old leaves which have served their purpose fall off the trees to make space for new fresh leaves. Leaves are like pages of a book.

My purpose for writing this book is to inspire people to live a life from their heart, from a place of love and courage. To have the courage to be free to be who we are meant to be in this lifetime. To live our dharma

---

[1] Mother Teresa. https://www.goalcast.com/2017/04/10/top-20-most-inspiring-mother-teresa-quotes/

INTRODUCTION

and highest purpose. Courage to "be" in the flow, and experience the highest form of expression our soul is here to experience. Our soul is our fuel, like the air we breathe. Our body is merely the physical vehicle that carries our soul. Our head is the steering wheel, our brain directs the wheel. Our heart is the compass. The compass follows the stars, the sun, the moon, and our intuition, to guide us through life.

I aim to share the message of love and courage with the world. I aim to remind humans that life is an evolution and it comes in cycles. Birth and death are a natural process of the life cycle. Each life is temporary; nothing stays permanent as we evolve, shed our skin, and move forward onto a new cycle.

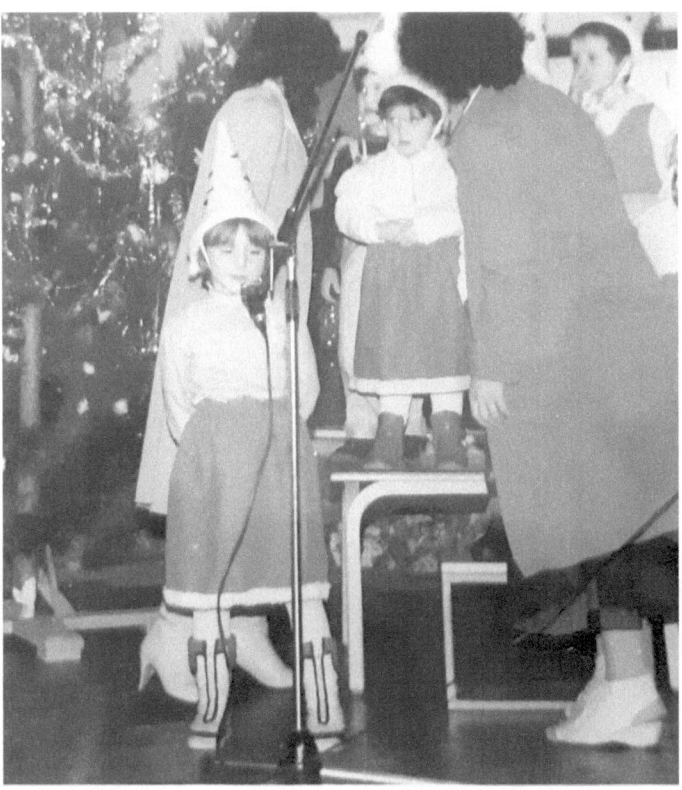

Maya in kindergarden reading a poem at a
New Year celebration performance

CHAPTER 1

MY FAMILY

My Father

My father Gorgi, or George, has been a great teacher and an influential person in my life.

The first thing he taught me was compassion and that there are no mistakes, only lessons.

He was the first person to teach me anti-discrimination towards people's cultures and race, equality, and ethics. He also taught me to have generosity, kindness, courage, to be honest, to love beyond boundaries, and to be fearless. My father always encouraged me to put myself out there in the public eye. I was on stage at school performances, dancing competitions, the local newspaper, as well as radio and TV shows.

My father is an engineer and he is the most reliable and trustworthy man I know. His word is his bond: he always does what he says and he is always on time. He is a family man who was home every day after work during my childhood. He is a man of integrity, honesty, and courage. He is a wise man.

He is a great storyteller like my grandmother, and, in their honour, I share my stories.

My Mother

My mother's name, Snežana, means "Snow White." I have always admired my mother for her beauty, her creative talents, her generosity, her kindness, compassion, independence, strength, courage, and her sweet, caring, and gentle soul. I could not have asked for a better mother. In my eyes, she is perfect in every way. My mother inspired me to be a free spirit, to dance, to sing, to create art, and to love unconditionally. It is through my mother that I discovered my healing powers and learned to trust my intuition. When I was little, my mother would cure me by using "rakija" which is pure alcohol on her hands and give me a full body massage. My sickness disappeared within minutes.

As an adult, I also found that my mother's touch had instant healing abilities: when she touched me, all my pain disappeared. So, I figured if she has it, I have it. I tried it and it worked. I have used energy and touch-healing on people and animals successfully.

My parents are warm and generous people. I remember one of my birthdays, maybe eight or nine: my mother made a large tray of baklava, which is a sweet pastry dessert with walnuts and honey syrup. She asked how many children were in my class. I told her 31. She cut the baklava into 32 diamond-shaped pieces, one for each child and the teacher. On the day of my birthday, I asked my teacher if I could spend 15 minutes to celebrate my birthday. Our classroom was an old-school, traditional classroom, with wooden tables in rows of about eight. I individually delivered a piece of baklava on a napkin to each child as they were seated at the desks, starting with my teacher. As advised by my parents, to every child I said, "poveli" which is equivalent to making an offering and each one replied with a thank you. Once I finished sharing the baklava, I invited the entire class to my birthday party at our house that evening. Most of the children came. My mother was a great cook and made a delicious cake and baked many sweets and savouries. I remember this was the best birthday I had in my childhood.

My birthday party

My Sister

My sister, Natasha, is four years older than me and lives in New Zealand with her husband and two children. I visit my sister and spend time with my niece and nephew at least once a year. My sister is my rock. She is a real inspiration for me. She is a strong, grounded, and independent woman. She is a great mother – one of the best mothers I have met – and this really inspires me about her. My sister is a humble woman. A quiet achiever. I feel she deserves to be acknowledged for her quiet but strong spirit, as she is mysterious in many ways.

Me and my sister

CHAPTER 2

MY CHILDHOOD

When I was a little girl, one of my favourite things to do was visit my grandparents: my dedo Borče (grandad Boris) and my baba Dafina (grandma Daphne).

They were my father's parents and played a big role in my life, especially my baba Dafina.

I remember two things about her. When I was two or three years old, my dad used to leave me with my grandmother who looked after me for a few hours a day. I spent most of my time singing and dancing in front of the mirror. I felt so happy and free to sing and dance and my baba allowed my expression to shine and glow. She bought me a skirt known as lambada skirt: it was baby blue and yellow, and, when I used to dance and turn, the skirt would lift up like a lotus. It was my favourite present from my baba and I continued to dance throughout my childhood.

The second thing I remember about my grandmother is her "jufki." It is a pasta similar to the Italian pappardelle. My baba used to make handmade jufki and dry them by hanging them around the kitchen. She would then cook me some fresh jufki and serve them with hot olive oil and fresh homemade goat's cheese. It just melted in my mouth. It was my favourite food to eat for breakfast, lunch, or dinner. There was no such thing as McDonald's or takeaway shops in the time I was growing up, so I enjoyed the delicious homemade meals my mother and grandmother made every day. As a treat we got a burger from the burger shop or a pizza at a pizza restaurant once or twice a year. Having a Coke or ice-cream was a real treat for me which I had only once or twice during summer school holidays. Eating freshly prepared home meals together as a family every day was very important in my life growing up.

My grandparents left Skopje and retired in the family holiday house in the mountains in a little village called Višni. In English, it means "sour cherry;" I guess because there were many sour cherry trees there. I used to love eating them and drinking sour cherry juice. I also love the colour of sour cherry: a red wine colour, which is my favourite.

As a child and teenager, I spent my summer and winter holidays there, as well as family gatherings such as Easter and May Day, which is equivalent to Labour Day. In winter, there was beautiful snow and it became a popular skiing destination. I remember making snowmen in our garden with my sister.

My grandparents had animals, mainly goats (and baby goats, which were my favourite), a cow, chickens, pigs, and a cat. We drank fresh goat's milk and ate fresh, homemade goat's cheese. Most of our food came from their garden and my dedo made red wine as well.

My dad was the youngest of three children. I used to spend my school holidays in the village with my sister, my cousin Daniela, who is one

MY CHILDHOOD

year older than me, and our youngest cousin Borče, who has the same name as my grandfather.

We would sometimes bring my favourite rabbits to the village as well. I loved my rabbits. We had a garden full of rabbits and I spent most of my free time after school with the rabbits.

The village was 7 km up the mountains. It was a long drive on the windy roads going up and around until you reached the top. Down from the mountain is the beautiful lake Ohrid. It is the largest and most famous lake in Macedonia and attracts a lot of tourism. You can find nice little cafés, bars, and restaurants along the beaches of the lake and eat fresh trout.

The water in the village was very cold and refreshing. We used to spend time with friends we met in the village, going for walks in nature and along the rivers, picking and eating the wild strawberries and hazelnuts. Sometimes, we walked to a little church on the top of one of the hills and lit a candle.

My sister and I loved watching movies and dramas. I used to enjoy watching the movie "Lassie," and Turkish or Indian movies, as they were always about love and the battle couples had to go through with their parents to fight for their lovers.

When my grandparents got older, they retired in a small apartment in the town of Struga, about 200 metres from the lake. I used to visit them every few years. We lived in New Zealand at the time. My grandmother and I would sit for hours on the couch as she told me the stories of her life. She was a great storyteller and certainly had a very interesting childhood. Sadly, she passed away in 2009, on Valentine's day, and I didn't get to hear all of her stories. I wish I had compiled a book of all her stories. This is the reason I am writing this book. I want my future children and grandchildren to know who I am, who I was. Knowing your ancestry helps people with their identity, confidence, and inner knowing. If you have this from a young age, you build a strong identity and you don't wander the world like a lost soul. At least, this is my belief.

Family gathering at the village with my grandparents

CHAPTER 3

MY SISTER AND I

My sister and I played together as kids and I am so grateful to have had a companion like her from the moment I was born.

My father encouraged us to do everything together, regardless of our age gap. When my sister was seven and started going to school, my father bought my sister a school bag, books, and stationery; he also bought me a school bag with books and stationery.

My dad, my sister and I. My sister's first day at school

When my sister was first learning how to read and write, I was there with her learning how to read and write too. My sister was seven when she started, and I was only three. Before I started going to primary school, my father kindly asked the school teacher if I could accompany my sister at her school and sit with her during her classes for a few months. My sister was about nine or ten and I was about five or six when I started going to school with her and sitting with her at her desk. We used to sit at the back with her friends. I got to know her friends and we all played together during the breaks. When my sister came home and did her homework, I would sit with her and do my own homework (which my father created for me). I therefore became advanced in my schooling. Before I even began primary school – which, in Macedonia, is at the age of seven – I already excelled in reading, writing, maths, and geography. When I was four years old, my family relocated for work from Skopje to a small town called Makedonski Brod, which translates to "Macedonian ship," and this is where I started my primary education.

I loved reading books and writing short stories and poems. I used to send my stories to the local newspaper and read my poems at performances in school. I was excellent in all my subjects and always came first in my class. I won awards and books. I used to write letters to other girls around the country (pen-pals, I think they call it) and I made my own envelopes with pictures from magazines and posters. I loved writing with different coloured pens. In Macedonia, we have the Cyrillic language, and you can write with all the letters joined so it looks artistic. It is a calligraphic style of writing. Nowadays, we write on our computers and iPads, and, sadly, we don't use the traditional method of writing very often. When I started writing my first book, I specifically chose to handwrite it and then transfer it onto the computer. I purchased a few beautiful notebooks and I have a pen with my name on it, which I carry around with me everywhere I go in case I feel inspired to write. This book is largely a compilation of my journals.

MY SISTER AND I

Fear, Love, and My First Healing

One evening, I had an accident. It was the only accident I had as a child where I got physically hurt. My sister and I went out to the park. It was after supper so the time would have been around 7-8 pm. My father would only allow us to go out in the evening if we went out together and stayed together. That was the rule. Going out in the evenings meant going downtown to the park by the river where most kids and young adults would hang out until about 10-11 pm in the summer. It was about a seven-minute walk from our apartment. The evenings were full of people, walking up and down the main road, hanging out in the park, getting ice-cream, or a soft drink.

My sister met her friends in the park and we separated. I went to play with my friends from school and she went to play with hers. This was against my father's rule because we didn't stick together and look after each other that night. What happened next is my first childhood trauma and the first lesson of my childhood. I am writing about this and relying on my memory – which is pretty good, as this happened 30 years ago. It is healing to write about past traumas and let go of the memories attached to it.

I was with my two girlfriends in the park and we heard some of the boys from school approaching us. It was dark, probably about 9 pm. Fear got the best of me and I started running. "Run!" I said to my friends. "Follow me and run." I took the lead. As I was running, I felt myself flying and falling. I was actually unconscious when I landed on the floor but I remember the flying part. I woke up to the voice of my best friend, Marija, calling my name and crying. When I opened my eyes, Marija was next to me, comforting me. I found myself at the bottom of some steps in a construction site. It was the back of a famous restaurant at the park, and they were building an underground discotheque within the same building. At the time of my accident, it was just a hole with a wall about three metres high. Now, the same place where I landed is the entrance to the discotheque and there is a big star there on the floor at the entrance. I visited the place when I was 18 years old: my first trip back to that small town after leaving at the age of 12 for New Zealand. Actually, the club opened just before we left, and I had my farewell party there. I invited all my school friends to join me for a dance party. For most of us, it was the first time we had entered a disco. There, we had a soft drink or iced coffee and had fun listening to music, dancing, and enjoying our friendships.

Having woken up from my first accident or fall, and coming back to consciousness, I found myself lying on the ground on my tummy with my left cheek on the ground. I had hit my nose and the left side of my face was covered in cuts and grazes. I also hurt my knee and my elbow, but my face was my biggest concern. My nose was bleeding for about an hour. It took me some time to move. With the help of my friends, I started to walk. Marija went to find my sister and about ten minutes later my sister arrived. Nobody could believe what had just happened; it all happened so fast. I felt like I had woken up from a dream. I felt like I was walking on another planet. I was too afraid to go home, fearing the response of my parents. I wasn't ready to go home yet. I wanted to get myself cleaned up and hoped I didn't have to tell them about the accident. I wanted to turn the time back, but I couldn't.

We went to the restaurant bathroom to clean myself up. I was shocked at what I saw in the mirror! The left side of my face was covered in blood and cuts… my right side was perfect. I couldn't believe this was me in the mirror. I covered my left side with my hand and only looked at the right side to remember who I was. I was shocked and I was scared. There was no way I could hide this from my parents. I was worried about telling my parents and risking getting my sister into trouble for not staying with me and looking after me as per my father's rule for going out in the evenings.

One of the friends suggested I see an old lady who was a healer, so they took me there. She was in her 70s and she got me to lie on the bed and she performed an energy healing for me to take away my fear. After about 45 minutes of the healing, I was ready to go home and face my parents.

Our apartment door was locked. I rang the bell, and waited for my parents to open the door. I was expecting their response to be negative; I was expecting them to yell and be angry at me and my sister for being home so late. But instead, to my pleasant surprise, their response was not anger. Their response was compassion and genuine concern. They were calm, and sincerely showed how much they cared for me. Their calmness made me feel calm and more at ease. I remember feeling very loved and cared for by my parents as they hugged me and looked after me until I recovered.

CHAPTER 4

NEW ZEALAND ADVENTURE

When I was 12 years old, my family emigrated to Auckland, New Zealand. I was in the middle of my fifth year of school. We left the country with one suitcase each, leaving our fully furnished apartment with all my childhood memories, books, clothes, and toys behind. We were all very excited about this new adventure and living in what looked like a tropical paradise. I completed high school in Auckland and we lived in a suburb called Lynfield. I discovered I had a flair for languages, so after high school, I went to university and studied a certificate in Spanish for one year.

I learned how to drive when I was 15 and got my driver's licence. I also got my first job as a checkout operator in the local supermarket Pak'n'Save in Mount Albert and bought my first car with my first month's salary. It was a black Mazda. Next, I really wanted to study travel and tourism, however, I didn't have enough money for the course which was taught through a private university. I started working full-time. I didn't want to ask my father for the money as my parents had just bought a new house and I wasn't familiar with the government support options. At the age of 18, I got my first office job as an Operations Assistant for a large international shipping company "Maersk" and got lost in the world of oceans for the next seven years. This was the start of my corporate career. My office was located in the tallest office building in Auckland on the 39th floor overlooking the Port of Auckland. I could see the big blue ships owned by Maersk coming in and out of the port. It was all very interesting to me.

At the age of 19, I purchased my own brand-new apartment five minutes from my parents' house and moved out of my parents' house for the first time. I was in a relationship and got engaged (but this relationship was to eventually end after nine years together). The apartment was nice: it had a small gym, a swimming pool, and a tennis court. I loved playing tennis. One year later, I sold the apartment and built a brand new three-bedroom home with my fiancé. I was only 21 at the time. I also had a black and white rabbit called Leo whom I loved very much. Leo was a free-roaming rabbit living inside the house. I was amazed to discover the intelligence of a rabbit during this time and how easy it was to house-train them like a puppy.

I worked for seven years at the shipping company Maersk and studied a Bachelor of Business part-time in addition to full-time work. My company paid for all my education. I became a manager at the age of 22 and the company transferred me to Sydney along with a promotion as Area Claims and Risk Manager. For the next two years, I lived in Sydney in a nice suburb called Chatswood. I worked full-time and studied again in addition to my work. This time, I was studying a post-graduate diploma in maritime law and international trade. After two years in Sydney, and finishing my post-graduate studies, I began a new adventure: I moved to London.

NEW ZEALAND ADVENTURE

Me in Auckland, 16 years old

CHAPTER 5

LONDON CALLING

I packed two suitcases and left Sydney in July, 2007. I had signed up to complete my master's degree in maritime law in London which began in September that year. First, I spent two months with my family in Macedonia, reconnecting with my roots. Then, at the end of August, I travelled to London to look for a job. I sold my house in Auckland and used this money to pay for my education and travels.

After I arrived in London, I took three different trains to meet with the director of a company for my first job interview. It was a case handler role for complex maritime claims for a company representing international insurance companies. I found the job through a recruiter in London. I emailed him while still living in Sydney and told him I was coming to London in three months and was looking for a job relevant to my studies in maritime law.

The company director was very impressed with my work experience and education, and offered me the job on the same day. He then kindly drove me back to the airport so I could travel back to Skopje and pick up my second suitcase, which I had left in Macedonia as I had been there for the past two months. I only came to London for the day to attend the interview.

Within a week, I was back in London. I found myself an apartment, started my new job, and my evening studies at London Metropolitan University. Life was busy and exciting. In the first year, I was fully focused on my job and completing my master's degree, which I completed with a distinction. I remember leaving for work at 6:30 am each morning, working until 4 pm, heading straight to the city for my evening classes from 6 pm to 9 pm, going home, having something to eat, and going to sleep. My weekends were spent studying and writing my thesis, exploring the city, shopping, and making new friends.

I remember arriving at the university at 6 pm for my evening classes after a long day at work and my friend would ask me: "How do you look so good and fresh after having worked all day? Where do you get the energy from?" My friend wasn't working like me; she was a full-time student and she said she spent all day sleeping and then came to university still feeling tired. It was an eye opener and a compliment for me hearing that. I never really thought about it. I was so used to working full-time and studying my qualifications on the side (as I'd been doing for the last seven years), that it was my normality and I didn't know any other way of life. I had never been only a student or only a full-time worker: I always did both at the same time. The nights were usually when I did most of my assignments, and often I stayed up until 3 am. My dad called me the night owl.

When I finished my master's degree and got some free time, I started reading personal development books. I was especially interested in improving my relationships with people.

Before I left for London, I was in a relationship for nine years, from the ages of 16 to 25. When that relationship ended and I decided to make the move to London on my own, I wanted to heal and learn what I could do to improve my flaws which I identified during the relationship.

I started reading all the books by John Gray, starting with, "Men are From Mars Women are From Venus," as well as books by Allan and Barbara Pease, such as, "Why Men Lie and Women Cry," and "Why Men Don't Listen and Women Can't Read Maps." I had fun reading these kinds of books for the next six months.

After becoming an "expert" on relationships, I wanted to learn how to improve my relationships with people at work and how to be a better manager. I was a manager from the age of 22 to 25, and during that time I was very much focused on achieving goals and meeting targets. One day, one of my staff told me that I should provide more positive feedback and not focus so much on what needed to change and improve all the time. I realised that was true. I was too focused on achieving goals and improving things, rather than recognising and acknowledging all the effort that was already being done.

After this, I started reading books on personality profiling, positive psychology, NLP (Neuro Linguistic Programming), astrology, and one of my favourite books, which was life-changing, "Emotional Intelligence" by Daniel Goleman. After reading this book, I realised I was so focused on IQ over all these years that I needed to start using more of my EQ. And it worked. I was making friends easily and had virtually conflict-free relationships at work.

The next phase was focused around my health, nutrition, and spirituality. In the evenings after work, I started attending health and nutrition seminars, and read many books about nutrition. My favourite was, "Eat Right For Your Blood Type" by Dr Peter J. D'Adamo. Following the guidelines in the book, as an "A" blood type, my diet recommendation was a vegetarian diet. This was already congruent with the change of diet I had implemented shortly after I arrived in London. This was actually instigated after I got very sick after having a filet mignon steak at a nice French restaurant; after that experience, I could no longer eat red meat. I took that as a warning sign, and rightfully so! The research I did on a diet suitable for my blood type was to avoid eating red meat.

One of the best spiritual books I read and implemented in my life was "The Four Agreements," by Don Miguel Ruiz, a Toltec Master of Transformation.[2]

The four agreements are:

1. Be impeccable with your word
2. Don't take anything personally
3. Don't make assumptions
4. Always do your best

These were simple agreements created with self which significantly improved my life once I started to implement them.

My second favourite spiritual book was "The Monk Who Sold his Ferrari" by Robin Sharma.

I found this book particularly interesting because the man was a lawyer who was working very hard and long hours, which led to him having his first heart attack. This was an awakening and defining moment for him, so he sold his house and his red ferrari and went on his spiritual journey to the Himalayas to meditate and heal himself. He came out as a rejuvenated, refreshed, and healthy young man. This book was particularly inspiring for me because I realised that becoming a lawyer wasn't the only option I had in life and that life choices and lifestyles are plentiful.

---

[2] The Four Agreements. A practical guide to personal freedom by Don Miguel Ruiz with Janet Mills

LONDON CALLING

During a conversation with one of my girlfriends in London, she said to me, "Stop being so negative and believe in yourself!" These words kick-started the next chapter of my life. I didn't want to be perceived as a negative person so I started my quest for how to be positive and believe in myself after everything life had thrown at me. I read the book "Ask and It's Given" by Ester Hicks, I did a short course on Neuro Linguistic Programming (NLP), and read some books by the Dalai Lama. I was on a self-healing journey and focused on improving my health, boosting my immunity, and getting to know myself better through spirituality.

CHAPTER 6

MONICA

I dedicate this chapter to my dear friend and flatmate Monica in London. I thank her for the friendship, the lessons, and the memories we shared in our beautiful apartment in the Docklands in London.

When I first arrived in London in September, 2007, I found myself a gorgeous studio apartment in the Docklands with views of the river. Coming from New Zealand and Australia, which are surrounded by ocean, I loved water and it was important to me to be near any water feature I could find in London. The river and the docks were the main options.

It was a brand-new, fully furnished studio apartment, with a very large living room and bathroom with a big bath, a large balcony, a laundry room, and a separate kitchen. The room was large enough to have a bedroom, a study, and a living room all in one. My typical day was going to work from 7 am to 4 pm, going to the gym, studying, or going to university, and having a hot bubble bath before going to sleep.

I had my first winter in London and my first Christmas alone without family. After about nine months of living in London, I became very sick with tonsillitis and had to take myself to the nearest hospital in a taxi. I was living alone and I didn't have any friends in the area, so I had nobody to ask for help. I found myself in a hospital for about a week and used that time to reflect on my life over the past year; I came to the realisation that life alone in a new country with no close friends and family wasn't easy. I had met many new friends in London, but I didn't have a close friend living in my area as they all lived in other parts of London.

I decided to look for a flatmate and move to a larger apartment in the building next door.

Monica had seen my advertisement and contacted me regarding the possibility of sharing a place together. I explained to her that I had found a gorgeous, large, two-bedroom apartment. One room had an ensuite and the other room had a bathroom with a bath. There were two balconies, one on each side of the building: the front balcony overlooked the dock and had beautiful views of the water. It was on the eighth floor of a brand-new building. The apartment came fully furnished. My room – the larger room – had a beautiful, wooden queen-size bed with a nice quality memory foam mattress, the largest built-in wardrobe I have ever seen, space for my study desk, and an ensuite with a shower. The living room had a large TV and a gorgeous, curved eight-seater red leather couch. This really attracted me to the place because I love red and I love the smell of leather!

I told Monica I was looking for a nice, professional lady to share this apartment with. We met at Starbucks in Canary Wharf. She seemed like a nice, quiet, and polite lady with a fashionable style, so we agreed to share the apartment together.

The next six months were an adventure and I became close friends with Monica. I was still completing my master's degree at the time so I would spend my evenings and weekends writing my final thesis. Both Monica and I had full-time jobs, so we spent most of the days at work. When we came home, we liked to enjoy a nice dinner together and maybe a glass of wine now and then. I wasn't a big drinker, and would only ever have one or two drinks.

In September, 2008, it was time for graduation as I had completed my master's degree in maritime law. I didn't have anyone to come with me as my close family lived in New Zealand. I felt sad that I didn't have anyone to share this special moment with, and Monica asked if I wanted her to come with me, however, that meant she would have to take time off work. I really appreciated the offer but I said no. I didn't want her to take time off work to come to my graduation. So, I went alone and met some of my classmates there.

Monica sensed I felt lonely during my graduation as I saw all my classmates with their parents and siblings, and I was the only one there alone. I was doing this degree for myself, not for my family or anyone else. By that time, I had become very independent and I rarely sought any help from my parents. I made the decision to study my master's and move to London all on my own: nobody had any input or knowledge of this until I moved there! I didn't want anyone to stop me or project on me their fears and doubts.

After graduation, Monica came home and gave me a graduation gift. I was astonished! Nobody had given me a graduation gift before; in fact, it was a long time since anyone had given me any gift at all. It was a pair of sparkling Swarovski crystals earrings. Wow! I felt so special. Monica always knew how to make me feel special.

I loved shopping for groceries and cooking, so I would often go to the shops to buy groceries and make delicious dinners for Monica and I. Monica would give me some money for the groceries as we shared the bills, and she would also throw in a tip like ten or 20 pounds for the efforts I made to get the groceries and cook the food. I loved that about Monica. I was impressed by this gesture and her showing appreciation that she valued my time and efforts.

One weekend, Monica was invited to attend a polo event when the Queen and Prince Charles were there. I had never heard of polo before. Monica invited me to go with her. She bought me a ticket and she also bought me a beautiful dress from Karen Millen (my favourite shop in London) to wear to the polo. I have to say, it was a very exciting day for me. It was all new to me and I didn't realise how glamorous this event would be.

After about six months living with Monica, I decided I wanted my independence back and moved out to a one-bedroom apartment not very far from our place in the Docklands. It was a brand-new apartment within walking distance to Canary Wharf. I loved Canary Wharf and it was my dream to live there. It reminded me of New York. Tall skyscrapers and most of the investment banks were there. It also had a nice, modern shopping centre where I used to go every day after work. All this was by the river where I could go for walks in the morning and evening. It had everything I needed. My apartment was in a building that formed a set of three. They were brand new buildings called Proton, Electron, and Neutron. I lived in the Proton Tower, which was the middle Tower on the 16th floor. It was right next to the DLR (Docklands Light Rail) station which took me to Bank Station in the city, straight to where my job was located, within 15 minutes.

My life was very convenient and comfortable at this time and I was feeling good about being in London. Everything was working out and I felt a flow of ease. I remember when I told Monica about my decision to leave, she was very upset and angry, however, she gave me a special gift. It was a beautiful little pink pen with Swarovski crystals. "Here," she said, "you can use this pen to sign your new lease for your apartment." Once again, Monica's little gifts and gestures melted my heart.

MONICA

Living in my new place, I missed Monica. We were still friends and went out for the occasional dinner now and then, but after about a year we lost contact. It's been over ten years since then and I still think of her. I really do value and appreciate the friendship we had and that's why I dedicated this chapter to her.

CHAPTER 7

MY SPIRITUAL HEALING JOURNEY

In November 2010, I experienced a spiritual awakening which led me to a career break for three years and my journey of spiritual exploration.

During this time, I was also questioning religion and having read books by the spiritual world leader Dalai Lama and "Living Buddha Living Christ" by Thich Nhat Hanh, I wanted to find out what was my calling and my dharma. I also read the first two books in the "Conversations with God" series by Neale Donald Walsch, which I found resonated with me at the time.

I remember waking up one morning to go to work to find I couldn't move my neck. I was frozen in my neck and the pain extended to the left side of my shoulder. I had medical insurance cover as one of my work benefits so I decided to go and see an osteopath. It was my first time visiting an osteopath and I didn't really know what it was. The first two sessions were ok but after that, I found it wasn't providing me with much relief; it felt like it was actually getting worse.

I continued going to work and university but I found it difficult with the pain. As the doctors couldn't help me, I decided to seek alternative therapy. I started acupuncture and had Chinese herbal remedies. This continued for about one year and, whilst I felt better, the pain was still there but had shifted from the neck and shoulder down to my lower back.

I couldn't understand what was happening; it was the first time I had had such an experience. I visited another Chinese acupuncturist and got a "cupping" session. It was painful but more effective than acupuncture at shifting the stagnant energy. The Chinese doctor told me it was a ball of stagnant energy causing the blockage and this ball was moving around my body. All I was doing was shifting the ball of energy around my body but it wasn't actually breaking it or releasing it.

During 2010, I also became a Zumba fitness instructor. I travelled from London to Athens in Greece to complete a two-day course to become a Zumba instructor. I enjoyed it and felt truly passionate and inspired by it. It was my chance to be creative and to do something I loved.

During the second half of 2011, I started to feel a deep calling to go back to New Zealand and to see my family. My sister had her two babies and I felt the need to connect with them. When I returned to New Zealand, it was August of 2011. I lived with my father in Hamilton as he had a three-bedroom house and lived alone. I visited my mum and sister in Auckland regularly. I felt freedom and happiness to have this break and spend time with family.

Me and my mum upon my return to Auckland in 2012

I think my father was happy that I was returning to live in New Zealand after seven years. We talked about me getting a car and he asked what kind of car I would like. I said a red sporty one. When I first left New Zealand, I had had a red sports car. It was an American brand called Saturn and I missed that car very much.

When I arrived in Auckland, my father greeted me at the airport. We went to the car park to find his car and we saw a red car, a Toyota Celica, with a large cardboard sign in the window saying "For Sale." My father said, "Look Maya, this car is for sale. Is this the kind of car you like?" I got excited and said, "Yes, yes! That's exactly the car I would like." He said, "Ok, sold," got out a key, opened the car, took the "For Sale" sign out, gave me the keys, and said, "Here you go, the car is yours." I was shocked beyond words. My father had bought me a car!

I didn't have a car when I was living in London for five years. I felt such freedom driving a car again in New Zealand. I enjoyed going for long drives and driving between Hamilton and Auckland to visit my sister and my mum. Whilst living at my dad's house, I would practice my Zumba every day and was preparing to start teaching some classes.

After spending three months in New Zealand with my family and not finding any work, I got a job in Sydney and moved back to Australia. Sadly, I had to give the car back to my dad and he sold it. I felt he was disappointed with my decision to leave. But I really struggled financially and missed the feeling of being independent. On the one hand, I was back in New Zealand with my family and had this great car which made me feel happy and free, but on the other hand, I had no income and I needed money to live and maintain my car. I also missed London, my apartment, and my friends.

I moved back to Sydney in November, 2011. I found an apartment in Dee Why Beach with a lovely lady called Megan. She was a school teacher and an Aries like me. However, three months later she decided to leave everything in Sydney and move to the Gold Coast to pursue her new career as a massage therapist. Luckily, I met some friends who lived on the same street – literally right across from the apartment I was living in! So when Megan left, I carried my bed across the road to my new room, where I stayed with a couple in their beautiful apartment.

I stayed there for another two months and really enjoyed my life. I worked part-time in the city at a clothing store, making enough money to pay my bills, and spent the rest of the time at Dee Why beach. One morning, I went for a swim at the beach like I did most days. Dee Why beach is a surfing beach so there were a few waves but it seemed calm that morning. After swimming, I turned around and started walking back towards the beach, when I was overtaken by a huge wave! I found myself under the wave, taking in water, and getting grazes on my legs. Nobody was around at the time, so nobody came to my rescue. This experience really scared me; I felt

I could no longer trust the ocean and I no longer wanted to live at Dee Why beach.

With Christmas and New Year's on the horizon, we got double pay working on public holidays and Sundays. I worked hard for a week and got enough money to set myself up for the next month so I could travel to Mullumbimby, near Byron Bay and attend the three-day Mind Body Spirit Festival which I had heard about by reading a postcard one day at a café. I was vegan at the time and regularly went to eat at the vegan cafés in Bondi Beach. I was obsessed with alkalizing my body, eating healthy organic vegan food, and drinking alkaline water known as kangen water. It was also during this time that I met my yoga teacher Marcus. I was attending his yoga classes at the gym in the city where I also was going to Zumba classes. My plan was to teach Zumba there in that gym and complete the personal training certificate required for me to teach. This, however, never happened, as I fell in love with Byron Bay and did not return to live in Sydney.

I was on a New Zealand passport living in Australia, which meant I was not entitled to any financial benefits and had to work at all times to support myself. I do not like debt. All my education was either paid for by me in cash or by the companies I worked for. I never got any loans. When I worked for Maersk in Sydney in 2005, they paid for me to go to the USA, for a short two-week course in UC Davis California. It was a beautiful little university town. At that time, I visited Seattle and San Francisco and my family who lived in St Louis: my uncle Slobo, who was a professional soccer player in America for 40 years, my aunt Linda, and my two younger cousins, Andrew and Lukas, who now live in San Diego. My uncle Slobodan or "Slobo" (which means freedom), was my mum's older brother and a big inspiration for me and my family. I admired his courage to follow his dream and move from Macedonia to America with very little money when he was only 18 years old. Sadly, my Uncle Slobo passed away at the age of 58, after getting an injury at one of his soccer games. He passed away doing what he loved. Rest in peace Uncle Slobo, you will always be my motivation, inspiration, and a guiding star. Until we meet again....

Me, my Uncle Slobo and my cousins Andrew and Luka in Saint Louis, USA

While travelling around Australia, I was still having pain in my shoulder, neck, and lower back, even after the osteopathy and acupuncture sessions. I devoted the next six months to researching and experimenting with different natural healing modalities.

Firstly, I did a five-day herbal detox combined with daily colonic irrigation treatments with my friend's mum in New Zealand, who is a naturopath. She has healed her own breast cancer through these detoxes and her story was very inspiring to me.

The detox was hard because I didn't eat anything for five days except soups and the special herbal drinks. The third and fourth days were especially tough and I was very emotional, as the detox was not only physical, but also emotional, mental, and spiritual. After day six, I felt great and lost about seven kilograms. I felt lighter, my skin improved, but the most exciting thing was I was able to feel so much in my belly than ever before. My intuition became stronger, and I started to really feel my body, my energy, and the energy around me. I felt I was on a completely different level, spiritually. This is the time I started listening to my body's needs and I ate what my body wanted to eat. I became vegan and drank a lot of green juices. I felt amazing and had so much energy. I felt on top of the world.

When I was in London, sometime in 2009, one of my friends suggested I see a healer located in one of the health shops in Chelsea. I love Chelsea; it's one of my favourite parts of London. I was apprehensive at the start and didn't know what to expect, but I took the chance with courage and had a session. This healer explained to me that every finger on his hand created a different effect when he touched my skin. I can't remember what all the things were but I found it fascinating. He asked me where the pain was. I told him it was on my lower back. He did this therapy on my lower back, pressing each finger for about a minute. And there it was! I felt all these different sensations with every different finger. At the end of the session, he said to me, "Go and have a glass of milk." I was very surprised by his comment. I had stopped drinking milk when I became vegan as I was under the impression that I was lactose intolerant. "It's ok," he said. "Your body is asking for milk, go and have a glass." I found the nearest Starbucks café and asked for a glass of milk. I felt good and my body didn't react how it normally reacts when I drink milk.

When I got home, I had all these emotional and energetic releases I did not expect. I went to bed and when I woke up, I felt like a brand-new person. I felt fresh, lighter, and more energetic.

Shen Therapy

After my first healing experience in London, I became fascinated with natural healing, so I started to explore and experiment further. I was usually guided by friends and word of mouth. I trusted the information and messages coming to me. I trusted the spirit guidance.

I found a place in London (I can't remember the name) but it was near Bond Street station. They offered shen therapy and the lady that attracted me was a Korean lady. She looked very young for her age and had amazing skin, a glow on her face, and wore a beautiful traditional Korean dress.

The therapists lived all together in the retreat centre where I had my sessions. It had clean and pure energy. The therapists don't live a normal life where they go out whenever they want in London. They only go out to the mountains in the Himalayas to recharge and collect new, fresh energy. Like a battery getting plugged in to charge, they were going to the mountains to recharge their pure shen energy, and return to do healing for people.

I found it so fascinating. I had a couple of treatments there. I explained to the lady that I was suffering from digestion problems and I had recently become vegan, gluten-free, and stopped drinking milk and dairy products. She said to me, "The key is to heal your gut, heal your stomach energy centre, and then you can eat whatever you want!" I said, "I can eat whatever I want? You mean I don't have to live with a restrictive diet forever?" She said, "Yes, once we heal your leaking energy chakras and fill you with fresh shen, you will produce your own shen energy, protect your chakras from leaking (losing vitality), and then you will have the necessary energy to digest any food you want!"

This was a dream for me. I was so interested in getting that result and being able to eat whatever I wanted, as I love food!

After having three shen therapy sessions, I slowly started introducing other foods in my diet. Now, I eat anything and everything in moderation. I listen to my body's needs and I feed it whatever it feels like eating when it feels like eating. I don't follow any diets anymore. I have freed myself from the belief that we need diets. Part of it is related to limiting beliefs and the other part is related to stored memories we had about food from when we were younger. It took about three years after that for me to start eating bread, meat, pasta, and sweets. I started reading about how childhood memories affect your reactions to food and how food allergies can be healed naturally. "The Power of Your Subconscious Mind," by Joseph Murphy is a great book I read during this time and I highly recommend it. I started practising self-healing methods using my brain, meditations, sun gazing, yoga, different frequency music, and my own body and mind intelligence. It was life-changing.

CHAPTER 8

SATURN RETURN AND LIBERATION

This chapter will reveal one of my major realisations and breakthroughs during my spiritual journey.

I was 29 years old when I made the big decision to leave my corporate career and my lavish lifestyle in the heart of London. After 5 years in London, I realised I really needed a break. I was studying my third law qualification in addition to working full-time, and so close to becoming a qualified maritime lawyer. "Maybe there is something else out there for me," my inner voice whispered to me, bigger than my corporate suit and high heel shoes, bigger than my office desk space. I felt a strong pull to go back to New Zealand and see my family.

After spending three months with my family in New Zealand, I started looking back at my childhood. What did I want to do when I was a little girl? What did I dream about when I was a teenager?

The answers were simple: when I was a little girl, all I wanted to do was sing and dance.

Unfortunately, I didn't have much of a singing voice (at least that's what I was told by my music teachers), so dancing became my main hobby.

It was now the end of the summer and the weather was starting to cool down. The rain started. I wanted more of the beach lifestyle and warm weather. This was the time I travelled to Byron Bay for the Mind Body Spirit Festival. By this time, I was only left with two suitcases of clothes and shoes. I sold or donated most of the belongings I'd brought with me from London: all those expensive European clothes and shoes I'd worked very hard to buy. I packed only one suitcase to take with me and gave away the rest of my stuff.

Here I was, on a one-way flight to Byron Bay, with less than $100 in my pocket and one suitcase of clothes and shoes. I felt like a gypsy travelling in style. I arrived in Byron Bay. It was a small and trendy little place by the beach. I liked it immediately. It was the first time in my life I stayed in hostel-type accommodation. I learned to share a room with strangers and make friends quickly. It was all very interesting and eye-opening hearing the stories of the people I came across. I thought I was the only nomad around. But Byron Bay was full of people like me.

I realised that I had been conditioned for so long to live a structured life. From a very young age, I had a structured life, a good corporate job, qualifications, stability, my own house, a nice car, savings in my bank. I had all of that before I was 23 years old. Now I was 29 and a nomad, travelling Australia with very little money and one suitcase.

At the festival, I befriended a girl who was a kundalini yoga teacher. She was from the United States and travelling around Australia teaching yoga. We started talking about crystals and I was fascinated to see how different crystals were making her feel. She was indeed a very sensitive soul.

SATURN RETURN AND LIBERATION

At the last of the three days of the festival, there was a big dance. I loved dancing all night, barefoot, wearing a long flowing dress. I felt so happy and free. It was a drug-and-alcohol-free event, and all I drank was water. I loved the feeling of getting a natural high. I was literally buzzing on air and water, dancing barefoot, and feeling the energy from the ground flow up my body into the sky. I had never felt happier and healthier and so connected to myself and my wild spirit.

The next day, I asked my new friend, Anya, what her plan was. She said she was going to a Hare Krishna community farm not far from Byron Bay. You get free food and free accommodation in exchange for helping out on the farm and learning about their community. I was open to exploring that. I was not very religious. My family grew up in Macedonia, where most people are Christian Orthodox, but my parents didn't practise much religion and never instilled any religious beliefs in me.

Perhaps this was the reason I felt so lost? Why didn't my parents raise me with any religion? Who was I? What was I? What were my values and beliefs? I had all these unanswered questions. I was accepting of all religions in the world and was open-minded about visiting the Hare Krishna community village.

We hitchhiked to the village. It was my first time doing something like that. I had had a car and a driving licence since I was fifteen years old – now here I was, 29 and hitchhiking! What in the world was happening to me? What would my parents think? So many emotions were going through me, but I felt so liberated, and so happy to share this journey with my new special friend. I felt a moment of safety and peace with her.

We arrived at the farm. We were given some basic accommodation. The beds were not very comfortable and there were spiders and bugs in the room. We had vegan food three times a day and Anya was teaching me kundalini yoga. We helped a little on the farm pulling out weeds, planting seeds, and feeding and milking the cows. I had not been on a farm since I was a little girl.

After moving to Auckland, New Zealand, I became a city girl. I lived mostly in Auckland, Sydney, and London in my 20s. When I looked inside my suitcase, I found I had nothing to wear on the farm! My fancy dresses and high heels I brought with me from London were certainly not serving me on the farm. I felt foolish. Here is this city girl, trying to live a life on a farm. Who was I kidding? I felt out of place.

Three days into the farm lifestyle and I was about to explode. I missed the buzz of city life. The people. The cafés and restaurants. The music. I felt so alone and disconnected. Straight after breakfast, I left the hall and started running down the fields, crying, looking for an escape, looking for a road that would lead me out of the farm. I was running and crying hysterically. I felt lost in my head without a plan, yet felt centred in my heart. My head was a mess, I was losing the plot, but I felt I was hinged on a pin at my heart and that's how I held myself together through the breakdown.

I sat down near a tree, metres away from a cobblestone road which I guessed was the path out of the farm. I didn't know where I was. I didn't know what was outside that farm gate. As I was sitting there alone, tears flowing down my face, a white ute drove past and stopped. A man in his mid-40s came out and approached me.

"Are you ok?" he asked. I looked at him, and started crying even more. "No, I am not ok," I said. "I feel so lost! I don't know what I am doing with my life anymore!" I said, crying. I had never spoken these kinds of words before. I was always known for having my life together and being organised. I always had it all together and now I was falling apart. Was I going through some kind of a mid-life crisis? Surely, I was too young for that.

"How old are you?" the man asked me.

SATURN RETURN AND LIBERATION

"I am 29," I replied, still in tears. I felt embarrassed. I felt like a big crying baby. This is not how 29-year-olds behave, I thought to myself.

He smiled and said, "Ah ha, don't worry! It's ok. You are just going through your Saturn return." He smiled confidently.

I looked at him, puzzled. "What?" I said. Well, that got my attention. I stopped crying and started listening.

He started explaining to me about the Saturn return cycle. The first major cycle starts between the ages of 27 and 29, and the second major one happens at the age of 57 or 58. He called it "the make or break" time of your life. People either become very successful and make it through life, or feel lost and start following the dark path of drugs and alcohol and suicide. "Look it up," he says. Most famous people either died at this age or became successful. He then told me his story and how he followed a girl from Australia to England. There he started to follow the "dark" path, until one day he started painting and painted a man shedding off his skin. "That's exactly what it feels like," he said, "like you are shedding your skin and becoming a new, rejuvenated person. It's when you really grow up and become an adult." It all made sense. I thought I became an adult when I was 18. Little did I know, I would be going through this at the age of 29!

After our little encounter, he walked away, got back into his ute, and drove away. I never saw him again. I didn't even know his name. He was a God-sent angel, that's for sure. He was the hero who saved the day and brought clarity into my life. I had never had a more interesting and educational conversation with a stranger before. I did my own research into the subject and found hundreds of articles and books which discuss the Saturn return cycle.

I got up and walked back to my accommodation. I found my friend Anya and I told her I couldn't stay there anymore and had to leave. I called a friend in Brisbane (another kundalini yoga teacher) who I met at the festival in Mullumbimby who offered his help to me if I was ever feeling "stuck." He agreed to come and pick me up and drive me back to Brisbane where I went to visit a dear girlfriend of mine who I had not seen for at least ten years. She lived alone with her two cats. I was excited to share my new story with her.

I picked myself up again and life started to make more sense after this experience. Life was flowing and I flowed with it. This was the time that I realised the value of having a conversation with a stranger. We didn't know each other. There were no rules. No judgment. No expectations. Two strangers, crossing paths, sharing their life stories. This is when I realised my life had a purpose: a bigger, more meaningful purpose than what I thought. This man was a sign-post in my life. The candlelight in the night. I would like to be a sign-post for other people too. I would like to be the candlelight for other people in their dark moments. I could guide other people from confusion and despair when they are going through their own Saturn return cycle. This is not something we learn at school, nor something that my parents could teach me. I wondered how many parents taught their children something like this. My deep, inner knowing told me that I had a purpose in this life to teach other people life skills that are not taught at school. It was up to me to spread the word. To spread the light. To share the love.

After Byron Bay and Brisbane, I headed back to Sydney to the Blue Mountains and attended a ten-day silent retreat called Vipassana. It was a residential retreat. Men and women were separated. We shared accommodation and delicious vegan food was provided. We woke up at 4 am each morning to practice meditation. After breakfast, we did more meditation and silent walks in nature. We had our meals without talking to anyone or looking them in the eye. I spent ten days like this. At the end of it, I was worried I would lose my voice for not having spoken for ten days. However, what I found was I spoke more softly, more slowly, and with purpose and intention. I now enjoy silent retreats and see great value in stillness and silence.

CHAPTER 9

RECONNECTING WITH MY INNER GYPSY ON THE GOLD COAST

A Call By The Ocean

Sydney started to get cold and I wanted to continue my summer adventures. My dream was to live in a hot place within walking distance to the beach. I was so over wearing corporate-style clothes for the last 10 years, that I donated most of my beautiful clothes and shoes to charity and sold some of the nicer stuff at a market stall at Bondi Beach. My garbage was someone else's treasure. I made one lady very happy when she discovered my beautiful Karen Millen clothes in great condition going very cheap. I didn't realise how expensive Karen Millen clothes were in Australia; I bought most of mine in London and sold most items for $50-$100, when each piece was worth $500-$1,000 here in Australia.

I had enough money for a one-way flight to the Gold Coast without luggage included. That meant I could only travel with one small bag so I left my large suitcase full of clothes at the airport to be donated to charity (the last suitcase of three I had left, after selling the other stuff). I was wearing my gorgeous white Tommy Hilfiger snow jacket and since I was travelling to a hot destination, I decided to get rid of the jacket as well. I was left with only one denim jacket now. I needed to feel light and free. I felt overwhelmed by any kind of burden.

The flight was about one hour long. I got off the plane and headed for the bus-stop outside the terminal to catch the local bus to Surfers Paradise. I was standing at the bus-stop waiting for the bus when I looked over to my right and saw a friend I knew from Sydney standing there. What a surprise! We said hello and were surprised to see each other there. It looked like we'd travelled on the same flight.

"What are you doing here?" she asked.

I said, "I came here on a one-way ticket hoping to find a job and stay here for a few months. What are you doing here?" She said she was visiting a friend and looking for the possibility of staying here too. She asked where I was staying, to which I replied, "I don't know, I was going to look for something when I arrived in Surfers Paradise."

"Well," she said, "I am heading to a friend's house near Surfers Paradise. I can ask him if you can stay as well for a couple of days."

"Perfect!" I said. I could not have asked for a better solution. The Universe had my back!

I ended up finding a job on the Gold Coast in the Surfers Paradise shopping centre – part-time three days a week – and I stayed there. I was working just enough to have money for bills and food and enjoying my life on the beach. I got myself a room in a beautiful apartment in Surfers Paradise overlooking the beach and everything was within

RECONNECTING WITH MY INNER GYPSY ON THE GOLD COAST

walking distance. I needed a long holiday to give myself a rest from the many years of hard work and study. My body desperately needed some sun and beach and that's exactly what I did for the next six months. I felt great. I got fit from all the walking as I didn't have a car, I got a tan, and looked ten years younger in no time. It is amazing what sun, beach, and a relaxing lifestyle can do for your body and mind.

The Gold Coast is a seasonal tourist place, so after the summer I lost my part-time job at the shopping centre and had to leave my Surfers Paradise apartment.

In London, in 2008, I had started to become interested in personal development and I wanted to explore the idea of becoming a life coach. I had already attended two short courses in London and read about 30 books including a short course on NLP (Neuro-Linguistic Programming), spirituality, and personal development. At the back of this book, I share a reference list of these books.

I was eager to continue this journey and I dreamed of becoming a life coach on the Gold Coast and living a life of freedom by the beach.

I attended a three-day personal development course with Chris Duncan and Regan Hillyer. After that, I started coaching people and preparing short workshops with the information I had learned over the last five years.

I loved empowering and teaching people I met along the way. I did life coaching in exchange for other things I needed, such as food and places to stay when I didn't have my own apartment. Sometimes, I also took money in exchange, but this was something I struggled with as I didn't know how to put a price on what I offered. I had never worked for myself before; I had been employed by companies since I was 15 years old, so I didn't know how to put a price on myself and my teachings. I was guided by my needs. Depending on what I needed at the time, that's what I would ask for. Most of the time I would charge

$80 an hour cash, however, there were times when I charged $200 or $500 cash because I needed money to travel to New Zealand and visit my family. What I charged for my life coaching sessions became dependent on my needs and values at the time.

In the middle of July, 2013, it was winter on the Gold Coast. The place became quiet and there was no work. I used the small amount of money I had from my coaching sessions and left the Gold Coast to spend time with my family in New Zealand. I stayed with my sister and enjoyed spending time with her kids.

A couple of months later, I decided to go back to the Gold Coast and try again. My mother gave me money to buy a one-way ticket from Auckland to the Gold Coast, which was about $200 at the time. I arrived at the airport and had no place to stay. I learned from some friends about something called "couch surfing" and decided to try that for a few days until I figured out my next steps.

I organised to stay at this place in Southport through the couch surfing website where I would get my own room for the night until I figured out my next step. It was free! Amazing! I took the bus to Southport and found the house.

A guy greeted me and I was shown to my room where I was to stay. It was someone else's room. I opened the door, and, to my horror, it was the messiest room I have seen in my life! The floor was covered with books, clothes, and all sorts of other things. The bed was also covered with clothes and other stuff. It looked very abandoned.

Where would I sleep? There was no room to move in this mess and it was dirty and filthy. "How can people live like this?" I thought to myself. And how can people advertise this room to other people? I was in shock. It was already 8 pm, I had no money, and nowhere else to go. I stayed there for the night, sleeping with one eye open. When the morning came, I started my next adventure.

RECONNECTING WITH MY INNER GYPSY ON THE GOLD COAST

I met a lovely lady called Karen who had a spare room to rent in a lovely peaceful house. Karen was in her 50s and the house was large and spacious. I explained to Karen that I desperately needed a place to stay, but I didn't have any money at the time. However, I could offer my services in exchange until I got a job. I explained to her I was a life coach and I could share with her some of my teachings. Karen was also into personal development so we had nice interesting chats during my stay there.

Within a week I found another part-time job and that covered my rent to live at Karen's place. I liked living with Karen and she was very flexible with me coming and going as I pleased, but I didn't have a car and I wanted to be close to the beach and shops. I liked walking: that was my mission, to walk everywhere, stay fit, and have a healthy lifestyle.

I really wanted to continue my personal development studies and obtain a qualification to become a professional life coach and live the life of my dreams. I imagined having a beautiful office in one of those high-rise buildings overlooking the beach.

To make this dream happen, I decided to move back to Surfers Paradise so that I could be within walking distance to everything and meet people to offer my life coaching services. I had my first client who was paying me $80 an hour. It was a man I met at a bus stop. He had given me $5 as I didn't have change to pay for the bus and I didn't know how the bus cards worked as it was my first time catching the bus there. We exchanged numbers so I could meet him to give him back the $5. The next day I organised to meet him at Starbucks. I did as promised and brought with me a $5 note. He said, "Don't worry about the $5, I want to hear more about you and what you are doing here." He offered to buy me a coffee and have a chat. So, I explained to him about my dream to become a personal development coach and explained to him what I teach. "Ok, I will try it," he said. He was interested in booking sessions with me and I was thrilled to have my first paying client!

What were my lessons from these adventures?

- Trust
- Letting go of control
- Letting go of expectations
- Letting go of the need to be perfect
- Compassion and understanding of people through experiencing life in their shoes

Part of me was comforted because I saw the other side of how other people lived. It turns out life isn't as perfect as I was raised to believe it was. My father was a very clean and tidy man and wanted everything to be in order and have its place in the house so he could easily find everything "with his eyes shut" as he would say.

My grandmother, my mother's mum, was a hoarder and my father always used to tease her for being a gypsy and a hoarder. "Did you know you are part gypsy?" my dad would say to me. He didn't elaborate on what being a gypsy meant, so I grew up with the impression that being a gypsy was a bad thing and that being messy like my mother and a hoarder like my grandmother was also a bad thing. I grew up in an environment where I set myself very high expectations and standards of being perfect like my father, or at least his definition of "perfect:" to be clean and tidy, to listen to teachers and elderly people, and to be good at school. In other words, to be obedient, a people-pleaser, and always put other people first. I think he probably got that from his parents. I mean, who wouldn't want their child to be a little, obedient version of them? I guess many parents do, but not me: I will make sure that my children have the freedom to be playful and expressive, not a conditioned version of me. Practising letting go of control and expectations is something I will consciously do when I become a parent.

The more I travelled and stayed in different people's houses, the more I learnt about the outside world and the different types of people, personalities, and cultures. Eighty percent of the houses I stayed in were very messy and some of them were so messy that you couldn't find a free spot available on the floor; the entire floor would be covered with all sorts of stuff. Messiness beyond my imagination!

I started to feel more at peace with myself and grew more love and compassion towards my mother and my grandmother. I realised that creativity equals messiness. It is ok to be messy. The brain requires messiness in order to be creative. I read a couple of books on this as well and I sighed in relief. I was grateful that I had a messy, creative mother who was teaching me so much.

This experience has given me not only greater understanding and compassion for my mother and grandmother but it gave me more self-love, as I was growing to love these aspects in myself too and learned that it was ok to express this side of myself which hadn't been expressed before.

I started fully embracing the gypsy in me! I was wearing colourful clothes and long, flowing dresses. I was travelling without any plans and being spontaneous. I was dancing Latin and belly dancing travelling around Australia. I started painting and created some beautiful pieces of art. I am so grateful for the gypsy in me and for all the gifts I have been given.

UNVEILING THE PATH TO HAPPINESS

CHAPTER 10

LOST IDENTITY, NEW IDENTITY

May, 2015
Moving to Melbourne

While living on the Gold Coast, I often travelled to Brisbane and Sydney to dance salsa. I was obsessed with Latin dancing at the time and danced four to five times per week. This kept me fit, happy, and young. Dancing is one of the main ingredients to a happy, healthy, and youthful life. I danced since I was a little girl and it has always been a big part of my life.

I had just returned from a short trip to New York after a dear friend of mine, my next-door neighbour in London, treated me to a return ticket there and three nights' accommodation.

My friend was there on a business trip from London and suggested I come along to see New York. I stayed in a hotel on Seventh Avenue in Manhattan and had my own room. I had dinner with my friend on one of the evenings and the rest of the time I was on my own shopping and exploring New York City. It was winter and pretty cold, especially coming from the summer on the Gold Coast, so I didn't go out at night except one evening to watch the musical Chicago. After watching Chicago, I had dinner in a lovely Italian restaurant/piano bar, Da Marino. I really enjoyed the evening. I went alone to the restaurant and the staff and management of the restaurant were exceptionally nice to me and very friendly, so I didn't feel alone at all. There was a man playing the piano and the restaurant was so cosy and so traditionally Italian. I only paid for my main meal: the drinks and dessert were on the house! They really were lovely and treated me so well. At the end of the evening, the manager of the restaurant walked me to my hotel to ensure I was ok. I said goodbye to the man when I arrived at the main door. I didn't even know his name and never saw him or New York after that evening. I later found out this restaurant was quite famous for celebrities and featured in the movie Sex and the City. According to their website, "It is the house of love, the living room of artists and the taste of Italy. Pure Magic!"[3]

My flight home was via Sydney, so I stopped there for a few days. I went to my usual night club to dance salsa. It was a Tuesday night, and I had been going to that place for a few years now and had got to know a lot of the usual dancers. I left my bag on the sofa and proceeded to the dance floor. I had a great time dancing for a few hours. It was just after midnight when I wanted to leave. I went to the couch to get my bag but it was missing! As I had just come back from New York, I still had my passport in my bag, along with my wallet, all my cards, a Chanel eyeliner I'd just bought in New York, my essential oil Green Goddess, and a few other small but meaningful items. Who would steal my bag? I reported it to the police and two policemen came to the scene. A few friends from the club helped to try and find the bag but found nothing. We all

---

[3] www.damarino.com

LOST IDENTITY, NEW IDENTITY

gave statements to the police and went to get something to eat. My friends treated me to a meal that night.

I felt as if I had lost myself and my identity in Sydney, but I was embarking on a new journey.

Melbourne was my next (and now final) destination!

I needed some ID fast and tried to get a new driving licence in Sydney, but as I had a Victorian driving licence issued in Melbourne, I couldn't get a licence in Sydney. I had some distant family in Melbourne and a couple of friends that I thought could be able to help. This was now extra, unplanned expenses, and I didn't have much money left or a place to live. I booked a one-way flight to Melbourne on the 3rd of May, 2015. It was almost winter and all I had was one small bag of clothes from the Gold Coast, which was not suitable for the Melbourne weather. I arrived in Melbourne and called a friend, explaining what had happened and that I needed some help. I borrowed some money: enough to get a new driving licence, three day's accommodation at a hostel in St Kilda, and some food. I chose to stay in St Kilda because it reminded me of LA with the beaches and palm trees along the streets.

After my three days at the hostel and spending the money I had, it was time for a new manifestation. I needed to make a plan for what to do next after getting a new driver's licence. Should I go back to the Gold Coast? Winter was coming and there was not much life or work in the Gold Coast in winter, so I decided to try my luck in Melbourne.

I needed to get a new passport to replace the one which was stolen. I needed a job, fast. I met some girls at the hostel who worked in a nearby bar and they suggested I come and ask for a job there. I worked at the bar for a couple of weeks and made enough money to get a new passport and a flight back to Auckland to spend time with my family and decide what to do next in my life. The passport arrived on the same morning on the day I booked the flight, so that was another lucky manifestation by me. Slowly, slowly, I started rebuilding myself again and felt at ease once I had a new passport and a new driving licence.

After visiting my family in New Zealand, I returned to Melbourne and decided to change my life and find stability again. As I had spent the last three years on planes, living out of a suitcase and travelling, I wanted to stop these adventures and get grounded. Losing my passport and identity cards had given me a bit of a shake-up and I didn't want to experience that again.

I got myself a job back in the corporate world, working as a claims manager for the same shipping company Maersk where I used to work for before I left for London. This company always had a special place in my heart and I was so grateful for the years of experience and all the travel I did working there. In the seven years I worked for Maersk before moving to London, the job took me to business trips in Singapore, Copenhagen in Denmark, Bangkok, San Francisco, Seattle, UC Davis in California, Hamburg in Germany, Rotterdam in Holland, London, Antwerp in Belgium, and Bratislava in Slovakia. Whilst living in London, I visited Trieste in Italy (where my grandmother and mother used to travel for work in their younger years), Norway, Istanbul in Turkey, Madrid in Spain, Granada in Spain, Paris and Aix en Provence in the south of France. My favourite places were Aix en Provence and Cassis in the south of France. I remember swimming in the freezing cold Mediterranean sea and it was so refreshing.

CHAPTER 11

DARK NIGHT OF THE SOUL

December, 2019
Melbourne

I took the train to work most mornings and walked over the bridge in Southbank. Crossing the river, I often saw homeless people busking for money. There was one man that I always saw on the bridge with his little white dog and it melted my heart to see him hugging his dog and keeping him warm inside his jacket. The love and connection they had was so profound. This was a homeless man who had very little financially but had a big heart to be looking after an animal in need. Even a homeless person can find meaning and purpose in his life and help someone in greater need than himself. This is inspiring and takes real courage.

It brought back memories of some of my tough days I experienced when I was living in Queensland. There were days I did not have a home and occasionally slept on a beach. I was too embarrassed and too proud to tell people of my situation. I was afraid of being judged. I had no energy to stand up for myself and ask for help. So instead, I withdrew. I hid inside a cocoon until the rough seas were over. Some call this enduring the dark night of the soul. It requires understanding of the anatomy of our spirit, prayer, and patience.[4] Based on my experience, it is during this time we receive our greatest courage, find our inner power of our spirit and insights about moving forward in life. This is how I connected to my inner genie or wisdom and learned about trust, patience, and faith. This is not something you learn from a book, but must experience in itself. It is like a part of the human soul is shedding: a part of me was dying and a new part was being born.

In fact, the lessons I learned being without a physical home were the best but toughest lessons of my life. I remember one day, I arrived in Melbourne from the Gold Coast with very little money. I walked on one of the bridges in Southbank and saw a homeless man begging, so I gave him my last money I had in cash. I felt that he needed it more than me. I was in good shape and good health, I had my confidence and trust that if I shared my small wealth with others freely and from my heart, I would receive what I needed for the following day. I had complete trust in the Universe that I would be protected and cared for.

It was true. The next day, I got a job and started earning money for myself. In many cases, help came at the very last minute. I would wait for days and hours for something to happen, with the Universe really testing my patience and trust – and then, at the last minute, help would come.

My advice for my readers is: don't start arguments and violence over money or physical things and petty little things that don't matter. This is why people become homeless in the first place. They have enough of family violence and the strong ones choose to leave the house and toxic relationships behind and start living life on their terms. They

---

[4] Anatomy of the Spirit. The Seven stages of power and healing. by Dr. Caroline Myss

go out in the real world and in nature and master their life skills and spirituality. They connect to their inner power and wisdom. This is how I learned about trusting myself and the Universe or God. These lessons would not have come to me if I didn't have those nights where I slept on a beach under the stars. I put myself in those situations so that I could learn things the hard way. Compassion and empathy is something you learn by having your own experiences and putting yourself in the shoes of others.

The planet Earth was my home, the sky was my protector. My body was my home, first and foremost. We maintain our bodies like we maintain a house. We keep our bodies in shape and good health. We decorate our bodies with clothes and jewellery and accessories, the same way we decorate our physical houses. Therefore, our body is our first home where our soul lives. Some say our body is the vehicle for our soul. Others say, my body is my temple. Many of us like to have quiet enjoyment and peace within our human bodies which we call our home.

If we don't feel safe within our own home, how could we feel safe outside it? Having attachments to physical things and money for safety is not a healthy way to live. Many people live like this. They need houses and money to feel safe, they need the doors and windows locked to feel safe, or they even need security guards to be safe. Earning a lot of money is one choice of having a good life but not the only choice.

When I was growing up in Macedonia, I remember that my family, especially my mother's side of the family, never locked the doors of their houses and always left the windows open for fresh air. Friends and neighbours were always coming and going as they pleased. The doors were always left unlocked even at night. If I was going out at night, I would come home at 3 am and just simply walk in. There was no key! In fact, when I first arrived in Macedonia to visit my grandmother at her lake house when I was 25 years old, I went out 'til late with friends. I had forgotten to ask for a key. I arrived at the house, saw one of the windows was open, and I climbed up to get in through the window. I then went to check the main door and realised the door was unlocked and I could have easily just come in through the door. I didn't have to climb in through the window! I didn't even check the door, I just assumed I needed a key to get in and that the door would be locked during the night. Everyone was sleeping inside the house peacefully. Feeling safe and at peace within yourself in your own body is the greatest gift of all. Trusting your soul to guide you and provide for you, for what you need, when you need it, is the second greatest gift of humanity.

Learning to trust, learning to live from a place of safety, and learning how to ask for help, were the lessons I got from my time spent in Queensland. I remember on the first day of my arrival in Brisbane I was verbally assaulted by a police officer over a misunderstanding. He was very manipulative and aggressive, forcing me to admit to something which I did not do. I experienced the misuse of power of the ego from this police officer and it did not give me a very good impression of Brisbane. From the moment I arrived there, I knew it was not going to be an easy chapter of my life. But I carried on…. with courage… stepping into the unknown. I have become a wiser and stronger person as a result.

CHAPTER 12

MY PSYCHOSOMATIC THERAPY JOURNEY

I attended a Mind Body Spirit Festival in Brisbane in 2013. As I was walking through the hall, I noticed a lady looking at me. She was offering face readings. I had never had a face reading so decided to try it. It was very profound and some of the things she said brought tears to my eyes. I left the stand feeling like a different person. I felt like something was cracked open inside me. I had been "seen." She asked me if I wanted to book a session with her. I took her business card and left. Her name was Bianca. I remember one thing I learned in the session which stood out to me, "the issues are in the tissues," and that certainly was true at the time as hundreds of tissues were filled with my tears.

I don't remember the last time I cried in front of another person. I went to the bathroom, crying some more and washed my face before continuing my journey at the festival. My next stop was a Hawaiian lomi lomi massage. I had three people giving me a massage at the same time. It was the most amazing experience I have ever had. My body felt like it was floating on a cloud. My face was down during the massage, and my tears were flowing freely. I was crying so much there was a small pool of tears on the ground. I had never cried during a massage before. I felt like something had burst open inside me and I was letting out all these trapped emotions I didn't know I had.

I felt a lot had happened to me emotionally, mentally, and spiritually in those three hours at the festival. The next day, I found the business card that Bianca the face reader gave me and I booked an appointment with her which was held at a wellness centre in Brisbane.

I had no idea at that time that Bianca would play a significant part in my life over the next three years as she became my teacher. I flew to Melbourne a few times to study a Certificate III in psychosomatic therapy with her. I am not going to go into too much detail here, as that journey warrants a whole book in itself, but I will reveal that studying psychosomatic therapy opened up a whole new world for me and made me a very different person to who I used to be. I became a lot more in touch with myself, my emotions, and my connection to my body and mind. It took my spiritual journey to a whole new level. I became a qualified practitioner in 2015 and worked for six months at a natural healing centre in Eltham in Melbourne, practising this therapy and witnessing changes in people's lives.

I was holding half-day workshops and shared my gifts and wisdom with others through my teachings. The main reason I started studies in psychosomatic therapy and coaching was to help my friends and family. My friends were always coming to me with their problems, and it felt like a natural thing to do. I was always the one listening to their problems and holding space for them. In the last ten years, I have helped many friends and strangers without charging anything for my time and effort. This was my contribution to humanity and making the world a better place. I wanted to show people that kindness and love still exist in the world.

MY PSYCHOSOMATIC THERAPY JOURNEY

"Heal The Woman Within Retreat" with Evette Rose Ubud, Bali

After completing my certificate in psychosomatic therapy in Melbourne in 2015, I decided to continue the journey of healing and psychosomatic therapy and attended a six-day healing retreat with the lovely Evette Rose. I also purchased her book called "Metaphysical Anatomy," which contains root causes and explanations behind over 600 ailments and diseases. This book became my bible and I started to use it in my daily life to help me heal from any pain or disease I was experiencing.

The retreat was amazing. I met other women from around the world, gathered together to heal our journeys in Ubud, Bali.

I loved Ubud and the resort where we stayed. Every day we had teachings, yoga, and meditation with Evette. After the day was finished, I would get a massage and eat nice, healthy, vegetarian meals. The place was very peaceful and I was awakened by birds and roosters singing each morning. On the second to last day of the retreat, we travelled to a healing waterfall for a blessing and we all went inside the waterfall, the cold water falling on top of our head, cleansing our energy. On the last day, I received a deep healing and a blessing from a local healer and priest. During the healing, which was an energy bodywork session, as I was releasing loud noises of pain and power, which I call my roaring, the sky changed and there was lightning. "You are creating this change in the sky! You are so powerful," Evette said. It was such a magical, profound moment.

On the same day in the late afternoon, a few hours before we boarded our planes to leave Bali, me and another lady I met at the retreat decided to get tattoos to mark this profound experience.

I got a monarch butterfly on my left ankle. A butterfly symbolises transformation and rebirth, moving through different life cycles. This was exactly what I experienced after the healing retreat and I feel the tattoo represented the start of a new chapter for me.

CHAPTER 13

MY YOGA JOURNEY AND THE PATH TO INNER PEACE AND HAPPINESS

It all began with hot Bikram yoga, 90 minutes classes in a heated room of 38 degrees. It was an escape from the cold English winter. I love the heat; it relaxes me, so I started going to the classes every evening after work. It was very soothing and restoring for my nervous and digestive system.

I tried hatha yoga after that, but I did not like it as much as I liked Bikram yoga. When I moved back to Sydney in 2012, I met my yoga teacher Marcus. I felt connected to Marcus and felt calm, peace, and wisdom in his presence, as though we had met before in another life. I started attending his classes in Sydney and discovered a deeper connection to yoga and to myself.

In 2015, when I moved to Melbourne, I found a yoga studio in Balwyn where I met my teacher Susan. I fell in love with Susan's yin yoga class and started to regularly practice at the studio. The studio is run by Susan and her daughter Clare. After practising there for about 18 months, I decided to join Susan and Clare's yearly retreat to Hydra Island, Greece.

I now share some of my highlights from the retreat.

27 May, 2018
Hydra Island, Greece

It was a long flight from Melbourne to Athens via Doha on Qatar Airlines. I arrived in Athens and took a ferry to Hydra Island which took another one and a half hours. I arrived on the island and was greeted by Susan and Clare.

I settled in at the Bratsera Hotel on Hydra Island and went to have lunch, which was a salad of fresh tomatoes and feta cheese. It sounds so simple, but it was one of the best salads I had tasted in a long time. The tomatoes were so juicy and full of flavour, and the cheese was also incredible: so fresh and soft, it melted in my mouth. I have never felt so satisfied by a salad with only two ingredients. After lunch, I went for a walk around the island. I was headed for the port to look for donkeys as I really wanted to see a donkey.

On my way to the port, a shop caught my attention. I walked inside. There were beautiful clothes and a few paintings and homeware. I noticed a peculiar painting of a donkey. I started looking at it and then I looked at the owner of the shop and thought to myself that there was a resemblance between this painting and the owner of the shop.

He saw me looking at the painting, walked over to me and said, "Oh, that's my self-portrait!" I laughed. He was an elderly man in his 60s or even 70s, with greyish hair, a few missing teeth, and a long nose. He really did look like the donkey in the painting and he wasn't afraid to admit it. I loved his sense of humour and honesty.

He asked me where I was from and I told him I was from Australia. He said, "When we Greeks were learning maths and algebra, Australian people were still hanging from the trees eating nuts." I laughed. He said that I looked like a trustworthy and harmless person and he feels like teasing me because he knew I would not get angry or harm him. That was true.

He started telling me how the Greek people believe they invented everything and therefore feel they are owed something by the rest of the world. They feel they should be always taken care of, be looked after just for who they are, and for what they have invented and created over the years. That got me thinking: yes, we should indeed be looked after and provided for as part of coming to this planet to share our wisdom and help others towards the healing and raising of human consciousness.

I decided to buy a couple of nice clothes and negotiated a price for cash. He packed the items nicely in a bag and gave it to me. I said, "No you keep the bag here, I am going to the port to find the ATM and get cash out for you."

"No, that's ok," he said. "You take the bag and go. Come back after you have a coffee and get the money. Take your time, I trust you."

So, I walked out of the shop with a bag of two beautiful items that cost EUR 300 and I didn't even have to pay. Now, that was trust. What a beautiful, empowering feeling that gave me.

I walked to the port, had a coffee, and 15 minutes later I went back to the shop and gave him the money, as promised. I started thinking about the importance and meaning of trust and empowerment.

If you give people trust in advance, they have something to uphold, so they will do their best to keep it. My belief is that you have to give something first in order to receive it. If you don't give people trust and expect them to uphold something which you don't have in you and haven't given to them yet, you can't expect them to deliver back on your trust. The other person starts in the minus and has to work harder and longer to get your trust. There is no equality. I remembered my father when I was little would always say to me, "I trust you" before he asked me to do something or gave me something to carry or buy from the shops. It made such a difference to hear those words and feel the trust was already there and you didn't have to fight for it.

28 May, 2018
Hydra Island, Greece

I started this gorgeous day with an early morning meditation watching the sunrise on a cliff on Hydra Island. I love Mondays. I was born on a Monday, so it's always been a happy day for me. A fresh start to the week, inviting new opportunities, new dreams, and new creations.

As I was spending time with my yogi friends here on the island, I was learning to open myself up on a deeper emotional and spiritual level and accept intuitive guidance and self-healing.

My journey to the island started with me feeling ill on the ferry. I had motion sickness for the first time. I worked in the shipping industry for many years and was often exposed to oceans and ships. When I was 18 and started my career in the shipping industry, I was sent for a three-day experience onboard one of the cargo ships owned by the company. We travelled to three different ports around New Zealand. I did not have any motion sickness then. Why was I having motion sickness now? Having studied psychosomatic therapy, I started to analyse this symptom. What was changing in me on this journey? What was the motion of the sea stirring up inside me? My internal waters became turbulent and I knew I was going to get some shifts and answers on this trip. I was open to receiving guidance, love, and light. I was very happy to receive the light and warmth from the Mediterranean sun and get some medicine from the Mediterranean Sea. I have missed that so much.

29 May, 2018
Hydra Island, Greece

I woke up again at 5 am and joined the group on a walk to the cliff where we waited for the sun to rise and did our morning meditation. After the meditation, I jumped into the sea for a refreshing early morning swim. The water was cold but felt so refreshing and so rich in its natural goodness. They call the sea the best medicine in the world, and I can feel why. It was sensational.

After breakfast, we headed for a walk up to the mountain monastery, which is approximately 500 metres high. Once we reached the monastery, we enjoyed the superb views of the sea. As I was walking up the steps, it felt like the stairs to heaven, ready to be held in the palm of God.

30 May, 2018
Hydra Island, Greece

After our usual early morning meditation and waiting for the sunrise, we had breakfast and took a small boat to a beach called Bisti. We were hoping for some peace and quiet on this secluded beach, however, we were greeted by a few groups of loud English tourists, disturbing the nature and peace on the island. I could not comprehend why people travelled such a long way to come to a beautiful remote peaceful island, and instead of enjoying the peace and connecting to nature, they bring their noise and disturbance with them. I guess it takes time for people to transition from a noisy, loud city to a small, remote island. I can start meditating within minutes or even seconds of closing my eyes and connect to the place I am in, so I spent my afternoon relaxing on the beach, meditating, and writing in my journal. For me, it was important to connect to the island, to respect the island, its nature, and energy without feeling overpowered by external noise. I felt at peace and enjoyed the stillness.

Before leaving Australia, I had booked a flight to Skopje after my retreat in Greece, however, I decided not to go to Macedonia on this journey. I wanted my retreat to be the highlight of this trip. This is something I was doing for myself and it felt very special for me to be gifting this time to myself and my wellbeing. I felt I was shedding some of my skin here on Hydra and letting go of some childhood past which no longer served me.

Yin Yoga Training
New Year's in Bali

In the last week of December, 2018, I completed a yin yoga teacher training with my teacher Marcus. I did five days of yin yoga from morning to night and obtained my 50-hour certificate to teach yin yoga.

I really enjoyed it and learned a lot. It was the first time I had decided to spend the time between Christmas and New Year's doing something for myself. Usually, I am with my family during this time. On the evening of the 31st of December, after we finished the yin yoga training, I had a nice dinner with Marcus and his assistant from Japan, and they drove me back to my hotel on their scooter. That was really fun. It was three of us on a scooter driving the streets of Ubud, in Bali.

I spent New Year's Eve in Bali with myself on the balcony of my bungalow, watching fireworks in the distance, and came home the next day on the 1st of January, 2019.

2019 became the year of yoga for me.

I enjoyed the training in Bali and the retreat in Hydra the previous year so much. I loved visiting Greece, so I decided to attend another yoga retreat. This time, I attended the Blue Bliss Happiness Retreat on the magnificent island of Koufonisi with my new teacher, Apostolia. Here, I share some of the highlights from this retreat.

13 July, 2019
Koufonisi Island, Greece

I felt inspired to start writing again and reconnect to my deeper inner being and my higher purpose. I travelled on a 25-hour flight from Melbourne to the small island of Koufonisi in Greece for an eight-day yoga retreat with the beautiful and selfless Apostolia.

Embodying our spirit is about unearthing those hidden gems, those inner gifts waiting to be explored and shared, like a genie coming out of the bottle. Thank you, dear Apostolia, for holding the space today for me to express my true self, my fears, my doubts, my courage, and my love.

I felt that the Blue Bliss Happiness Retreat was my destination to self-discovery. I felt that after this retreat, I would be ready to embody my gifts and share my stories with the world.

I found beautiful, perfectly formed spirals on the beach and collected shells and rocks to bring back with me to Australia. The spiral is such a powerful healing formation. In Australia, we have the didgeridoo which Indigenous people use to create a long spiral of sound, which is very healing and calming.

14 July, 2019
Koufonisi Island, Greece

At 7 am, I woke up to watch the sunrise: to salute the sun, absorb its light, love, and warmth, and ask it for my daily guidance.

I love sunrises, especially after the retreat in Hydra last year when we woke up every morning at 5 am and walked to the cliff to meditate and wait for the sun to rise.

MY YOGA JOURNEY AND THE PATH TO INNER PEACE AND HAPPINESS

I never used to be a morning person and this is something in me that changed over the past two years as I attended more yoga retreats around the world. As my teacher, Apostolia says, "The sun is never too tired to rise, it rises every morning." I want to be like the sun. To spread love, warmth, and light to the world. To brighten up the day and shine light on the darkness of the world.

I often follow my favourite teachers around the world. I moved to London in 2007 after meeting my maritime law university lecturer, Susan. Maritime law was so much more fun and easy to understand with Susan. My yoga teacher in Melbourne is also called Susan and my mother calls herself Susan because not many people in New Zealand can pronounce her real name, Snežana.

I also moved to Melbourne from the Gold Coast following my teacher Bianca and now, five years later, I am still here in Melbourne.

My teacher, Apostolia, is a very special soul. She is so kind, loving, and generous. I imagine her as a mermaid coming out from the deep sea bringing medicine to heal me, or a jewel from the ocean bed, a very special gift shining like a diamond.

I extend my deepest gratitude to her for showing me there is another side to the world, the other side of the coin, that love and kindness still exists in the world, and for making me a part of her tribe, her global community, the happiness tribe.

16 July 2019, Full Moon
Koufonisi island, Greece

Circle
Celebration
Dance
Music
Fire
Stars
Sea
Birth and rebirth
Closure
Letting go
Welcoming the unknown
Courage
Taking a leap of faith
Support
Grounding
Completion
Integration
Love

17 July, 2019
Koufonisi island, Greece

Healing of the Inner Child

This morning, I experienced one of the best yoga classes with Apostolia and the group. We did a visual meditation and within seconds of closing my eyes, I was already up in the sky, floating on a cloud, with my spirit guides and angels around me. I could feel my ancestors. I had a peacock on one shoulder and a black cockatoo with a red tail on the other shoulder.

In the afternoon, I had a healing with Apostolia and we worked on my inner child healing.

I chose a song to mark this moment: "Heal the World" by Michael Jackson. Now, I sing this song to myself and my inner child whenever I need to connect to myself or when I feel lonely. This is to remind myself that I am never lonely, as I am always here with me.

As we were going through the healing outside in nature in the yoga shala, I heard the donkey singing. After the donkey, the geese also made a sound. It was beautiful to feel so connected to myself, to nature, and the animals on this island. I remembered a moment when my sister and I used to play as children. She used to be my donkey and I would ride her around the living room and make donkey sounds.

I found a heart made of marble with a keyhole in the middle of it. I thought, "What a perfect gift for my teacher Apostolia." So, I bought it for her and gave it to her on the last day when we departed Koufonisi.

18 July, 2019
Koufonisi Island

Connection to the rocks and nature

This morning, I woke up at 5 am to watch the sunrise with my yoga tribe. We walked to a cliff with some beautiful rocks and caves which I really enjoyed. I found myself connecting a lot to the rocks on this island. I was fascinated by their formation and colour, the way they all fit in naturally together, all the rocks supporting each other to form a larger cliff or a cave.

The water was a beautiful blue colour splashing off the rocks and in between the rocks forming little isolated private beaches and pools.

UNVEILING THE PATH TO HAPPINESS

Every time I put my hand on the rocks, I feel so much energy, so much wisdom, and so much memory.

I got very creative when I was by the rocks. I liked to sit next to them and write, collecting shells and small rocks. Memories came to me as a little girl playing on the beach. We used to travel to Croatia, Montenegro, and Bulgaria for our summer holidays as a child, and my favourite thing was to play with the sand and the rocks at the beach. It is interesting to note that nothing has changed about me here.

I still find the same things fascinating and interesting as when I was a child.

We watched the sunrise and did yoga on the rocks. After the yoga class, we played with our shadows on the rocks. That was very interesting, like watching the shadow of myself in a movie.

Some of the movements reminded me of a performance I did when I was a child. I was part of a theatre performance and played the role of a tree. I had to be grounded in my roots and only move my upper body by swaying my arms. I remember thinking, "I have such a small, insignificant role as a tree, I wish I played a bigger role in the performance." Now, as an adult, I realise the importance and significance of a tree: the importance of being grounded and moving our energy up through our body and through our torso and arms. It is actually such an important practise for our body and our energy. It took me 30 years to realise that.

On the way back, I went for an early morning swim at the beach before having breakfast. It was so refreshing and revitalising. As I was walking up the street to go back to the villa, I noticed the cows and geese sleeping. "Good morning!" I said. The cows then said, "Moooo" – good morning in their language. The geese then also said good morning one by one in their own language. It was such a magical moment to be so connected with everything around me.

20 July, 2019
Koufonisi Island, Greece

I can't believe I shared a room and became friends with a cockroach. It was sitting on the other side of the window every night when I went to sleep. The first day, I was afraid when I first saw it; I really didn't like cockroaches. The next night I saw it again with two little baby cockroaches. "Ok," I thought, "you are a mum and I will leave you there. Maybe you are there seeking safety and comfort at night." The cockroach was there every night I went to the room to sleep and I started talking to it. "Thank you for the company," I said. The next day, I decided to read about the meaning of the cockroach. What a profound message this was!

> *"It makes them the symbol for long life, refreshment, rebirth, and rejuvenation. Gives you a new perspective of yourself in line with your emotion, state of your mind, and spirituality… The cockroach is the gift for readiness and adaptability among others. When you see cockroaches in your dream, it denotes self-cleansing, renewal, and rejuvenation of your emotional, psychological, or spiritual well-being. After such a dream, you will need to re-evaluate your life."*[5]

---

[5] www.auntyflo.com/magic/cockroach

CHAPTER 14

THE PATH TO SILENCE AND INNER PEACE

25 October, 2019
Eremito Hotelito del Alma
Umbria, Italy

I have always wanted to travel to Italy. My grandmother and my mother spent time in the north of Italy when they were younger; my grandmother was working there for many years and took my mother as well before she got married.

I was super excited when I heard that my teacher, Apostolia, from Greece was holding a digital detox retreat in the forest in Umbria, which is between Rome and Florence. It was a six-day silent retreat in the beautiful hermitage hotel Eremito. I travelled 27 hours on a plane from Melbourne to Italy, via Doha, Qatar. Whilst on the plane, I was reading the book "Silence" by Thich Nhat Hanh which I really enjoyed and prepared me for the silent retreat.

UNVEILING THE PATH TO HAPPINESS

At Rome airport, I met up with the group. There were seven of us. I had come the furthest: the others were from Greece, Spain, and Switzerland. We all met at the airport on the morning of 25th October and got a shuttle together to take us to the hotel Eremito, which was about a two hour's drive towards Florence.

We encountered some unexpected challenges and adventures on the drive to Eremito which tested the group's communication, patience, and strength. The driver, who was Italian and spoke minimal English, decided to take a shortcut through the mountains (as per the instructions from his GPS) instead of following the main road around the mountain. Firstly, we got lost because we lost the GPS internet connection and phone signal, then the car broke down on a pebbled road in the middle of the forest.

We were trapped in the forest for about four hours looking for ways to get in contact with our teacher who was already at the hotel. We walked looking for a road, or a house, or any connection we could find to make a phone call. Finally, three of us, the youngest and fittest in the group, took a walk and the path of courage and hope to the nearest village. We found a house and decided to go in and seek help. A lovely lady opened the door, allowed us to use her phone, gave us some water, and chocolates. By this time, it was starting to get cold and dark and I was thinking of the worst: that we would be trapped in the middle of a forest all night!

Finally, just before the dark night arrived, the manager of the hotel came to our rescue and took us to the hotel in his 4WD. We arrived at the hotel tired and hungry. We had a nice jacuzzi bath and steam room session, followed by a delicious, three-course vegetarian meal in silence. By that time, it was 45 hours since I left Melbourne and hadn't slept in a bed for two days. I went to bed and slept like a baby.

I shared a room with a lovely lady called Sara who lived in Ibiza. I usually had a room for myself, but this time I decided to share my space and make a new friend. I couldn't have asked for a better roommate. She was beautiful, kind, considerate, and very zen – just what I needed.

The first three days, we had a silent retreat. Sara and I, although we shared a room together, did not communicate using our voice. We communicated in silence. Our group lunches and dinners were also in silence. This allowed for a better connection to self, greater awareness, and connection to our feelings and what we were doing. Eating our delicious vegetarian meals meant we could focus on enjoying and appreciating our meals and really tasting the food and focusing on self-nourishment, rather than focusing on making conversation. This silence was beautiful and peaceful. Everything I did was with flow and grace. I walked very slowly, paying attention to everything around me. The hotel was an old hermitage, transformed from an old monastery into a hotel. I liked the stone and wood it was made from. It looked very solid and very warm inside: intimate and cosy. All the food made in the hotel is vegetarian, cooked with love from all ingredients locally grown in the hotel gardens.

Being here at the Eremito Hotel brought back memories from my childhood in Macedonia. My grandparents' house in the mountains is a large stone house, similar to this place. Downstairs we had a living and dining room, a storage room where all the food and wine were kept, while upstairs were three bedrooms. Then there was a room where the animals lived. There were goats, a cow, pigs, chickens, and a little resting room. My grandparents also made all the food themselves, including red wine, goat's milk, and goat's cheese. We shared many family meals and celebrations in this mountain house. In the evenings, the youth in the village would gather at the nearby ex-army grounds and light a fire. Someone would bring a guitar and we would all sit around the fire in a circle singing.

It's exactly how we spent our evenings in the Eremito Hotel. After our silent dinners, we would have a sharing circle and then go outside and sit around the fire. Apostolia played the guitar and we would listen to her beautiful voice and join in singing together. I closed my eyes and was taken back to my childhood. The last time I had that experience in my grandparents' village, I was 12 years old. It was the last summer before we left Macedonia for good and relocated to New Zealand.

I started dreaming that one day I would transform our old family house in the mountains into a similar retreat centre and continue the family gatherings there, to continue the legacy and the life which my grandparents wanted for us, their grandchildren.

Me in Eremito, Italy, October 2019

THE PATH TO SILENCE AND INNER PEACE

26 October, 2019
Umbria, Italy

Our typical days in Eremito included waking up at 6 am and going outside for a walk. It was misty most days. I would have a glass of water with lemon, then at 7 am we gathered in the chapel upstairs for a prayer in both Italian and English. It was like music in my ears listening to the prayer in Italian; it is such a beautiful language. This was followed by an outside session of light stretching and breathwork, watching the sunrise. We then had a cup of coffee or tea and went to the yoga studio for our first two hours of yoga. It was the best yoga I have done in my life. After yoga, at 10 am, we had our delicious Italian breakfast outside in silence. The weather was always so perfect. It was autumn, and it was 20-25 degrees and sunny each day. My favourite food for breakfast was green vegetable juice and fresh ricotta cheese with fresh scrambled eggs and tomatoes. The bread was baked each morning and it was scrumptious – probably the best breakfast I have had in my life. Everything was fresh and made and served with love. I could really feel the beautiful energy, of love, peace, gratitude, and freedom. The hotel was the only place of occupancy in the forest, and all you could see and hear was nature. I had never before experienced such zen. I was able to quieten my mind, and have a deep inner rest.

After breakfast, we went for a walk in the forest and had a silent rest on the rocks nearby the river, listening to the sounds of nature. I could hear the birds singing. I closed my eyes and started thinking of my lovebird Mina. On the day I decided to come to this retreat, I got a lovebird which I called Mina. I saw her in my regular pet shop, swinging on a swing by herself, looking sad. I remember the week before I came to the pet shop, I saw two lovebirds together on the swing and I was thinking how beautiful and romantic it was. Now there was only one and she seemed sad and lonely. So, I decided to bring her home. I already had a parrot, a conure called Guchi, so I thought Mina could keep him company. I brought her home and let her fly freely around the house. I enjoyed watching her fly gracefully around. She was beautiful. She had the most beautiful, unique colours. I was very inspired by her and her wings, her freedom flying around the house. That was a Saturday afternoon and that moment I decided to take a leap of faith and book the silent retreat in Italy. I sent an email to my teacher to confirm to her I was going to join the group. It was my moment of freedom: I wanted to spread my wings and fly to Italy just like Mina. I enjoyed my days with Mina, especially being woken up by her beautiful singing in the mornings.

Three weeks later and only a week before I came to the retreat, I lost my beautiful Mina.

I put Mina outside in her cage on a table and she somehow managed to escape. I found her sitting on top of the cage. I opened the door to the house and waited for her to fly inside but instead she flew to the tree. Then she chirped and flew to the neighbour's tree. I then watched her fly away in the distance to another tree and lost sight of her. I heard and saw a big black crow heading in the direction to the tree where Mina flew to, and I ran outside trying to find her. By the time I found the house where the big tree was, it was already too late. I found the big black crow up on the tree branch holding my Mina in his mouth. I was being showered in her feathers. I tried to save her and I couldn't. There was nothing I could do and the crow flew away with my Mina in his mouth. I looked on the floor and I found Mina's beautiful tail feathers. She left me a gift before she went to the other side. I always admired her tail feathers. They were the colours of flames. I took the feathers and now keep them in a little box with me.

At our circle sharing at the retreat, we were around a tree in the forest. I shared my story of Mina with the group. We then together started singing for Mina. I dedicate this song to Mina and the forest in Eremito.

Dear Mina, thank you for giving me your wings
So I can fly to the forest.
Dear Mina, thank you for giving me your wings
So I can be here with my tribe.
Dear Mina, thank you for giving me your wings
So I can fly and see the world.
Dear Mina, thank you for showing me the way
to inner peace and stillness
Dear Mina, thank you for singing to me
Now I sing for you.
Dear Mina, thank you for giving me your wings
So I can fly to the sky,
So I can fly and reach the stars.

27th October, 2019
Umbria, Italy

This morning I started the day by watching the sunrise and absorbing the energy and light from the sun. This was followed by a yoga class which we completed with Apostolia playing the guitar and all of us singing together.

After breakfast we walked to the forest and came to a river where we did some blessing rituals, cleansing ourselves with fresh, cold water.

The white cat that lived in the hotel decided to join us on the journey. She followed us to the forest. She seemed to enjoy our company and liked sunbaking by the river. She was a beautiful white cat with green eyes who we named Spirit. She was our spirit guide. We all enjoyed cuddles with her.

I love spending time in nature. Watching the way the sun rays penetrate the forest is so magnificent. We spent about an hour in silence, meditating in the forest listening to the sounds of nature.

It was so beautiful and peaceful. It showed us how to be one with nature. That day, I really felt the connection and what it means to be in oneness with nature.

That evening, we set our intentions for the new moon. We wrote our intentions on pieces of paper for the following year. It's like making a contract with ourselves to make these things happen. One of my intentions was to have a family of my own. I wished to get married, buy a house, and have children. I also wished to use my gifts and creativity to offer help to the world. I wished to share my gifts with other humans, with nature, and the animals. I also had a dream to have my own retreat centre. I liked the idea of living in a community with the company of animals, and growing my own food. Something similar to this place, Eremito, and the zen lifestyle here.

This is a poem I wrote in Eremito and shared with the group at our circle.

You wanted to walk,
I gave you legs.

You wanted to write,
I gave you hands.

You wanted to sing,
I gave you a voice.

You wanted to dance,
I gave you rhythm.

You wanted to love,
I gave you a heart.

THE PATH TO SILENCE AND INNER PEACE

You wanted a vision,
I gave you eyes.

You wanted to be free,
I gave you a soul.

It's now up to you my dear child,
to use your gifts
and live the life of your dreams.

CHAPTER 15

PAST LIVES AND ANCESTRAL HEALING

23 November, 2019
Past-Life Regression Therapy Session, Melbourne

I went to the Mind Body Spirit Festival at the Melbourne Exhibition Centre. I love going to these events and supporting other creative angels who show their gifts on offer at this festival. I bought beautiful clothes, candles, books, crystals, pictures, and got some psychic readings.

One experience which really made an impact was the past-life regression therapy session with Paul Williamson.

He led me through a guided meditation to a memory of my soul many, many years ago. I felt like I was accessing something very deep and ancient within myself: a past life I hadn't tapped into before. I have tapped into some of my past lives but not one so deep and ancient.

I was a hybrid between a human and an animal, kind of like an ape but more a man than an ape. I am not even sure if that was an experience I had on Earth or somewhere else. I had a feeling it was not an experience on Earth but another place.

I was a male in my 30s. I had a beautiful wife and a child, a small boy. My wife was a much more developed human than me; she was beautiful with long hair. Our boy was 80% human-looking and she was about 70%, while I was about 50% human-looking. Our home was a beautiful home, an underground cave. We were a beautiful family, loving and peaceful and we loved our boy.

My wife had been kidnapped while I was at work. I left our boy at home and went looking for my wife. I was going down steps in a big underground cave led by guards. These guards were hybrids, big and tall men with wooden weapons and oil lamps.

Leading down to the cave was a big glass door that could only be opened by the guards and was very secure. I was told my wife was kidnapped and brought to the chief who was a huge hybrid. He was more of an animal than a human. I tried negotiating for my wife in exchange for gold. They said it was not possible: no negotiation of any kind was possible and I could never get my wife back. After trying everything I could to get her back, I was told she was no longer alive.

Devastated and heartbroken, I went back home. I went to see our little boy. He was about seven years old. I didn't say anything, just hugged him to comfort him. Suddenly, I saw this colourful light coming in the room through the window. It was a colourful, angelic expression of my wife. She hugged us both. She then joined us for dinner. She was an angel. I could see her clearly, she was just in a different form: a lighter form that could move around easier and quicker on her feet and fly. She was glowing and wearing a long colourful dress. She was with us every day. We continued to live life together and she always joined us for dinner, like she did when she was in her body.

PAST LIVES AND ANCESTRAL HEALING

We continued to live our life: me as hybrid man/animal and her as a hybrid angel/human. When I was old and in my 60s, I was lying on my bed; my son was grown up and had a wife, and they were both sitting by my side as I passed over. When I passed over, my wife was also there by the bed waiting for me and I flew straight into her arms. It was a beautiful experience. The most beautiful feeling of love and re-connection. I felt peace.

This memory confirmed to me my purpose here on earth. I am supposed to be a hybrid, living between realms. I am an Earth angel. I am here to teach humans about the afterlife and the connection with spirit angels. I am a living soul in a human body having an experience here on planet Earth. I have been here before, many times and in different forms, both human and animal.

I was so intrigued by my experience that I did some research about hybrid humans. I found a book by Bruce and Daniella Fenton called "Hybrid Humans" which I ordered so I could read more about similar experiences of other people.

> "Sooner or later … we have to accept the fact that all life on Earth carries the genetic code of our extraterrestrial cousins and that evolution is not what we think it is."[6]

I have had many other past lives: hundreds, maybe thousands more. The ones I most often see when I am soul journeying is when I was a gypsy travelling around the world with my mum, singing and dancing. I remember many trains and train-tracks. My mum was a performer and I used to travel everywhere with her. I enjoyed that life very much.

Another life I remember is living on a ship as a little girl. My mother passed away during my birth and I was raised by my father, who was ship captain, and by other ladies on the ship. I remember many

---

[6] Fenton Bruce, Fenton Daniella, "Hybrid Humans: Scientific Evidence of our 800,000-year-old Alien Legacy," (2018)

ladies, some young, some older. My father was not available very often. He was often sad and grieving over the loss of my mother. He was a drinker too. After my father died when I was in my teenage years, I remember getting off the boat with another lady and settling in a desert, I think in Egypt. There, I was a dancer and had a lot of gold. I had a good and wealthy life.

I also remember a life as a cat. I was a cat to a lonely old man. I had a couple of lives as a Native American Indian woman.

My belief is that we can have lives as both humans and animals throughout our many lives.

So, why are these past lives relevant?

We continue to experience the same issues and patterns in our lives until we heal and clear the blockages or learn the lessons. This could be an emotional blockage, a mental blockage, a physical disease, a pattern of abuse or superiority, a pattern of family violence, or abuse of power.

By identifying the issues in your past lives, you can gain clarity about why you are here in your present life: what are the issues that you need to focus on and heal? What lessons are you here to learn? What are your karmic patterns, or why are you in the same karmic relationships? Karmic relationships can be with the same person or swapping roles within the family circle. For example, in this life you may be the mother of a child, but in the past life you were the child. We take on the experiences of different roles and we choose our families. We may choose repeated lives within the same family circle but change roles or stay in the same roles.

This is why it's important to recognise the importance of each relationship you have with people in your life. To have respect and value for your children. They are not just your children who are inferior to you; they are here to teach you valuable lessons. Your child may be an old wise soul and may have been your mother or your grandmother in a past life and know more than you! Pay attention to what they say and what they do.

How do I know this?

My intuition tells me. My inner knowing or claircognizance is very strong. I am connected to and tuned into the universal intelligence and collective consciousness. When I meditate and listen to certain types of music, I connect to my past lives. When I listen to Turkish, Arabic, Spanish, or Native American music, I feel so connected to the music like I have been there before. I start meditating and see images and feelings from those lives. When I travelled to Granada in Spain, I started speaking Spanish without any trouble. I felt so free and comfortable speaking Spanish, as if I had done it many times before.

I will also share a story about when I was living on the Gold Coast and I first started to get these intuitive messages and dreams about past lives.

I was meeting a friend at the local Starbucks. I went there but my friend wasn't there yet so I took the empty seat next to this lady reading a book. She seemed like a nice lady in her 60s, wearing pink. I felt drawn to her. We started talking. She started telling me about the past-life regression sessions she had had recently and about some of her past lives. It was so profound. I was reading the book "Many Lives Many Masters" by Brian Weiss at the time and now, having met someone so randomly, I took this as a confirmation that it was real and does exist: it wasn't just my crazy imagination. She was a messenger and a gift to me from spirit.

Reading the book "Many Lives Many Masters" only reaffirmed things I already knew but had never spoken to anyone about. It was time for me to explore this further and embrace my gifts and wisdom. I started following the spiritual path more and more. I got some tarot cards and I offered free tarot cards readings to many people I met at cafés. They were very impressed with the messages they got and would often buy me a coffee or food to say thank you. I loved the exchange of energy and appreciation I felt.

CHAPTER 16

ANIMAL COMMUNICATION AND SELF-MASTERY

The first time I was introduced to animal spirit communication, I was on my way out of the Mind Body Spirit Festival in Brisbane. It was sometime in the middle of 2013. Having had a face reading and an amazing four-hand lomi lomi massage, I shed many tears whilst also feeling pain and pleasure. What more could I possibly experience on this day?

A woman approached me holding tarot cards and asked if I wanted an animal reading. I didn't really know what she was talking about, as I hadn't had a reading done before. I picked a card. It was the rabbit card. She said, "A beloved rabbit is sending you love and he knows how much he was loved. He misses you and sends you love." I burst into tears. More tears! I could not believe my ears. A few days earlier, I found out my rabbit Leo passed away. He was eight years old. Leo and I were very close and I looked after him for about five years until I moved to London in 2007. Leo travelled with me on a plane to Sydney when I relocated from Auckland to Sydney in 2005. He was a free-roaming, house-trained rabbit and I loved him more than anything in the world.

I felt awful for leaving him behind in Australia and not bringing him with me to London, but it was such a long journey I didn't want to risk his life. I missed him so much. This card really opened up my heart to something bigger: animal spirit communication is real!

I felt soft, subtle energy which connects us through other beings through our heart. This energy can be felt when you quiet your mind and become still in silence. The colours that resonate with the feminine heart energy are green and pink. I surround myself with these two colours, especially clothes I wear or items in my house, to help me connect with my heart centre. This heart centre also helps us to connect with other beings on the planet, such as the animal and plant kingdom.

In 2019, I attended a three-day workshop on animal communication by Trisha McCagh. I have used Trisha for consultations when I needed help with communication with my rabbits. I have also read her book "Animal Whisperer" which I found very interesting and was also pleased to read about other people who share my gift and passion.

Shortly after finishing the workshop, I felt a lot more connected to myself and the energy around me. I could feel the energy of the trees and plants, I could hear and sense what they were communicating to me. I have a better connection to my own animals and other animals around me.

I am here on the planet not just to experience a life in my human body but to master my life in my human body. I am on a journey to self-mastery and I am aware it doesn't happen overnight.

I knew I was a unique child from a very young age. When I started going to school, my bedroom had my study desk and library in it. I was exposed to all this knowledge from hundreds of books. At night when I went to bed, I would take a book which I needed to read for school or study for a test. I would open the book, look at the pages, close the book, put it under my pillow, and go to sleep.

Somehow, like a miracle, as I was sleeping, I was getting all this knowledge downloaded just like I was reading the book. The next day, I would go to school and just know all the answers. I felt so connected to universal intelligence, as though my body was downloading all the information I needed.

Now, I spend many hours a day meditating and downloading information or new programmes I want to introduce in my coaching business. Some people may think I am just in my room sleeping. But no, I am not just sleeping. I am meditating and downloading information from my Soul. This is how I get creative, come up with new ideas, and innovations. A lot happens in my sleep and during deep meditations. It is a very strange thing to explain to some people unless you have experienced it.

I am on a journey to self-mastery. I know how to do many things naturally and be guided by my inner knowing without having to do much training. I have done the training in my many past lives and I am here to share my many gifts and knowledge with the world. Especially, I feel very drawn to bringing humans and animals closer together, to show humans that we are part of the animal kingdom and all the special gifts we can get from mother nature and animals. I would love to explore shamanism more, especially plant medicine for our healing and communication with the animals and my spirit guides.

CHAPTER 17

INDIA

13 February, 2020
Rishikesh, India

I sat alone in my hotel room by the window, overlooking the Himalayas and the beautiful sacred Ganges river in Rishikesh, India. It is the holy place known around the world for its yoga and meditation teachings: the home of the deities, the sages, saints, and pilgrims. It is known as "The City of the Divine."

I held my clear quartz crystal in my left hand and started speaking to the Himalayan mountains in front of me.

> Dear God, dear Universe,
> Why am I here?
> Why India?
> What is my calling? What is my soul purpose?

I asked for clarity and divine guidance.

When I arrived in India, I felt my head crack open at the top. I could feel the energy of the Himalayan mountains on my head and face. The Himalayan mountains, especially the jewel which is located in Tibet, is the vortex of the crown chakra. This is the place to come if you want to expand your consciousness and connect to your Higher Self or "God."

When I was younger and had not started exploring religion and spirituality, I used to think God was a person. The usual impression people have of God is that it is an external powerful being. Many think we have to please God and that when we pray, we pray to God to make our dreams come true. We answer to God and make God happy with our actions so that we can go to heaven.

My personal self-discovery and spiritual journey has led me to believe that God is not external. God lies within us. It is a connection to our Higher Self. When I pray to God, I am actually praying to myself, to my Higher Self, and it is through my own conscious actions and responsibilities that my dreams manifest into a reality. It is all within me; it is in my own hands. Through prayer and meditation, I activate my self-healing and my superconscious, to transform or manifest my dreams into consciousness, or reality.

When I was in India, we did a lot of prayer and meditation with the Indian Gods. My favourites were Goddess Lakshmi for abundance, God Vishnu for protection, Goddess Kali for strength, and God Shiva and Goddess Shakti for love, which is the creative energy and balance.

What are we actually doing when praying to these Gods and Goddesses? We connect with their energy, their spirit or eternal being, and then we find these energies and qualities within ourselves. We are all capable of having what a God or a Goddess has. It is within our own power and wisdom. How to do that is what I was here to learn and master for myself, and then teach others how to do the same. When I first started self-healing in 2010 after reading the book "The Power of Your Subconscious Mind" and listening to various guided meditations and frequency music, I learned how to self-heal my body, my mind and spirit through lots of practise. I started to have vivid dreams and out-of-body experiences. I started to see, feel, smell, and hear all these new things. My self-awareness and that of the environment around me started to increase with my experiences. I started to sense danger and negative energy around me and used my senses to protect myself when I was travelling alone around the world. I started to feel much more confident in myself and my own power and intuition. Through yoga, breathwork, meditation, and having different life experiences, I learn to master my own Divine being and be the creator of my own personal life experience here on Earth.

My biggest lesson in India was learning how to surrender: to surrender to the Universe, to the Divinity, to my Dharma and Karma. I was seeking clarity on my life's purpose and mission. And what I received is to surrender to what is and what is to come. To have patience. To be patient with myself, to take care of myself, and learn to love myself first before I can love others. To expand my heart and expand my crown chakra so I can receive the messages from God and Spirit. To learn and experience oneness. And that I did through the practise of self-love, dance, connection to nature, yoga, breathwork, and meditation. Thank you, Mother and Queen India for the lessons. What a great start to 2020.

Me in India, Himalayas mountains cave

CHAPTER 18

SOUL PURPOSE AND REALIGNMENT

In January 2020, I joined The Coaching Institute in Melbourne to improve my coaching skills.

One of the main things I learned there is that when you are in alignment with yourself, you don't need motivation to go and do something or be something, you just become it. You live it, you embody it.

I decided to explore this concept further.

So, what does it mean to be in alignment?

I was guided to an online course called Soul Realignment by Andrrea Hess which uses the Akashic records. I have heard of the Akashic records before but did not feel guided to learn more about them until now. Soul Realignment uses Akashic record reading and clearing to help people understand and express their divine gifts and soul purpose.

A few nights before I found the course, and before I decided to enrol in it, I couldn't sleep and I was intuitively guided to search for Akashic records readings. I found a lady named Michelle in Melbourne and when I entered her website, the time was 11:11 pm. I knew I was meant to be there and that I was on the right path. When I made the payment online for my reading, the time was 12:12 am, which once again gave me reassurance I was doing the right thing. I was so excited for this new learning and could not wait for my reading which was booked for the following Monday. I was born on a Monday, so it is my favourite day of the week. It signifies new beginnings and new opportunities for me. When you love what you do in life, you love Mondays and cannot wait for them.

I was waiting in anticipation for my reading at 1 pm. I have had many psychic readings before but this one was different. I knew and felt in my heart that this was going to be memorable. I had given permission to another person to access my soul records and interpret for me what information they held. What a gift and honour that is.

I thoroughly enjoyed the reading which was very detailed and accurate. The main things I got from the reading were:

1. She said that I am here to teach balance and harmony to others and I may be drawn to public speaking. I agreed: I do like public speaking and I look forward to doing more in the future. She said my challenges are perfectionism and setting high standards, which can delay or deter me from getting my work out in the world. Again, this was 100% accurate.

2. She also said I am here to learn compassion and patience. She said I was grounded and have a close connection to nature. She said my challenges are in establishing good strong boundaries

and not letting people take advantage of my kind nature. Again, all these are 100% accurate and resonated with me.

3. She said I am part of the Starseed soul group which I already suspected based on my own research and that I had some lives on the planet Maldek which was a planet between Jupiter and Mars that was destroyed and now forms the asteroid belt. After its destruction, I had some lives on Mars before my many lives on planet Earth. She said I was a very old soul, hundreds of thousands, maybe millions, of years old.

4. Michelle also told me that in the afterlife I was a life review counsellor, helping souls with review of their life lessons. She said my spiritual gifts are in law and justice, organising, planning, project management and leadership, making things beautiful and functional, bringing structure, problem-solving, investigating, protecting animals, spiritual teaching, nurturing, and healing, and I would do well in acting and public speaking, if I so chose to.

5. My main lessons in this lifetime are perseverance, discernment, listening to and trusting my intuition, and finding balance. She also said I need to learn about my emotions and how to be connected to my intuition and emotions.

I thanked Michelle for the reading, and, after I finished the call, I did some research on the planet Maldek and it all made sense to me now. I had often remembered life on a green, prosperous, happy, and harmonious planet, and I often longed for a place like "home" which no longer existed. The Starseeds are deep and mysterious souls who come to Earth to perform acts of service for humanity and the planet and have a deep sense of knowing there is a bigger world out there. We are here to teach humans about that world and raise consciousness. Starseeds often devote their lives to their mission or purpose and many are restless until they find their true calling – myself included.

I have so many gifts and talents, and I am always on a mission to create something new or learn or teach something new. Having this sense of identity, purpose, and meaning in life is what brings me deep inner happiness and makes me fulfilled.

A few weeks after the reading with Michelle, I decided to get another reading, this time from a lady called Shelly. Shelly also told me I have had many lives on other planets before coming to Earth. She said Earth is like going to university for the soul. It is not an easy place to incarnate. Humans usually spend time on other planets where life is easier and more friendly. I definitely resonated with that. She also told me I was part of the Blueprinters Technicians Soul group. This soul group is like the engineers of the human experience. People from this soul group usually have jobs as engineers, doctors, business analysts, teachers, or entrepreneurs. We are more karmically tied to this planet than any other soul group and we need to learn more about our emotions and how it ties in with the human body experience and its soul.

After listening to this, I resonated with this. I started to access my own intuition and inner knowing about why I am here and why I incarnated on planet Earth. I often feel like I am a visitor on this planet or like I am undercover. I am very much focused on creating improvements in the human experience, perfecting and mastering the Divine human experience, helping raise consciousness and knowledge, and teaching people about integration of the body, mind, and soul. My focus is especially on the complexity of the emotional body, and the integration of our emotional body with the mind, physical body, and soul.

After having these soul readings, I signed up for the Soul Realignment certification course with Andrrea Hess and now I am a certified Soul Realignment practitioner and Akashic records intuitive reader to help other people when they need guidance about their Divine soul gifts and their life's mission or purpose.

SOUL PURPOSE AND REALIGNMENT

I'm hopeful that sharing my life journey and stories will inspire others to find their true calling or dharma, to find purpose and meaning in their own lives, and trust their own unique path to inner peace and happiness.

DREAMS, GOALS AND VALUES

THE NEXT FIVE TO TEN YEARS

My inner knowing tells me I am on a mission to self-mastery; to act as a medium or a bridge to teach others to find a balance between the material or physical world and the spiritual world; and to empower others to remove the mask or the veil to be seen for who they really are. My spiritual journey so far has taught me how to deepen the connection to myself, to trust my inner guidance and inner knowing, and to become aligned to my dharma or higher purpose and mission.

I have some goals and a vision I work towards and I will share them here.

I am also aware that the Universe doesn't give you what you want, it gives you what you need, when you need it, and when you are open and ready to receive it. Whilst I have these dreams and goals, I also leave the door open to other opportunities that I have not considered yet.

1. To be a respected successful leader, teacher, and spiritual master. I want to have my own successful business and have financial freedom and abundance for myself and my greater family.

2. To have a family of my own, and raise my children in a loving and peaceful environment.

3. To be a successful author, publish many books, and share my stories and knowledge with others

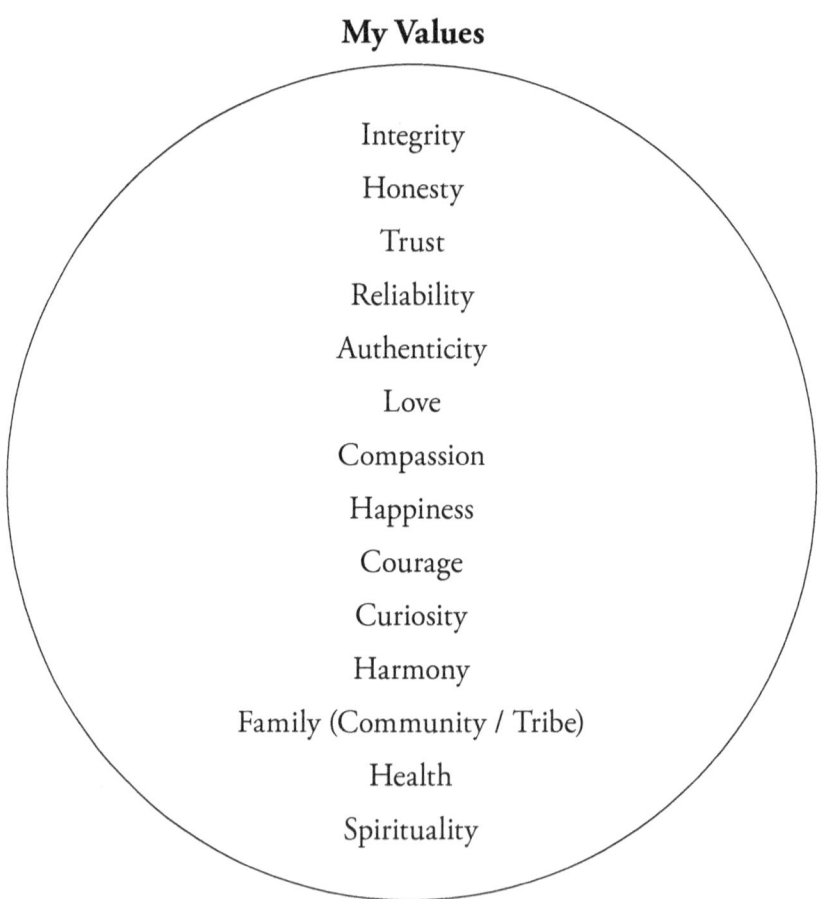

My Values

Integrity

Honesty

Trust

Reliability

Authenticity

Love

Compassion

Happiness

Courage

Curiosity

Harmony

Family (Community / Tribe)

Health

Spirituality

REFERENCES

My Favourite Books From My Spiritual Journey:

D'Adamo, Dr. Peter J. "Eat Right For Your Blood Type"

Dalai Lama, "The Art of Happiness"

Farmer, Dr. Steven, "Healing Ancestral Karma"

Gray, Dr John, "Men Are From Mars Women Are From Venus"

Gray, Dr John, "Mars and Venus on a Date"

Gray Dr John, "Venus on Fire Mars on Ice"

Goleman, Daniel, "Emotional Intelligence"

Hanh, Thich Nhat, "Living Buddha Living Christ"

Hanh, Thich Nhat, "Silence"

Hicks, Ester and Jerry, "Ask and It Is Given"

McCagh, Trisha, "Stories from the Animal Whisperer"

Michie, David, "Buddhism for Pet Lovers"

Murphy, Joseph, "The Power of Your Subconscious Mind"

Myss, Dr. Caroline, "Anatomy of the Spirit: the Seven Stages of Power and Healing"

Pau, Maria, "Kill your addiction before it kills you!"

Pease, Allan and Barbara, "Why Men Lie and Women Cry"

Pease, Allan and Barbara, "Why Men Don't Listen and Women Can't Read Maps"

Rose, Evette, "Metaphysical Anatomy"

Rose, Evette, "Healing your Boundaries, Finding Peace Again"

Ruiz, Don Miguel, "The Four Agreements"

Sharma, Robin, "The Monk Who Sold his Ferrari"

Silk, Danny, "Loving our Kids on Purpose"

Smith, Penelope, "Animal Talk"

Southgate, Natalie, "Chakradance"

Virtue, Doreen, "Earth Angels Realms"

Virtue, Doreen, "Assertiveness for Earth Angels"

Walsch, Neale Donald, "Conversations with God 1 & 2"

Weiss, Dr. Brian, "Many Lives, Many Masters"

William, Anthony, "Medical Medium"

Wolfe, David, "Superfoods"

ABOUT MAYA

Maya is a spiritual life coach, artist, creative therapist, traveller, and writer.

In this book, Maya shares her true story of finding inner happiness by following her heart, courage, and intuition, travelling around the world, and being the creator of her own life experiences. She shares her stories, wisdom, and knowledge to inspire and empower others.

Maya was born in Skopje, Macedonia and relocated with her family to Auckland, New Zealand at the age of 12. After Auckland, she lived in Sydney, Melbourne, Brisbane, Gold Coast, and London, England.

Maya takes us on a journey of her life experiences, travels, passions, and life lessons. Her passion and purpose is to bring balance and harmony to the world. She enjoys working with people to guide them to their true calling with the courage to pursue their own unique path.

To fulfil her mission, Maya has now launched a life coaching business called Lovebird Blessings, inspired by her beloved lovebird Mina. Further details can be found on www.lovebird-blessings.com.

Special thanks and gratitude to my partner and best friend Rob Darman and the Darman family who have been my family in Melbourne for the past five years.

www.ingramcontent.com/pod-product-compliance
Lightning Source LLC
Chambersburg PA
CBHW021154080526
44588CB00008B/338